5-

Dear Robin and Michael,

For your very first Merry Christmas

in Santa Fe — enjoy!

love,

Barb & Ron

Christmas Celebration

Santa Fe Traditions
FOODS & CRAFTS

RICHARD CLAWSON

Text by JANN ARRINGTON WOLCOTT

To Robin & Michael, Season's Greetings! Share in my delight. Jann Arrington Wolcott

CLEAR LIGHT PUBLISHERS
Santa Fe, New Mexico

Clear Light Publishers

823 Don Diego, Santa Fe, New Mexico 87501

LIBRARY OF CONGRESS CATALOGING-IN-PUBLICATION DATA

Clawson, Richard

    Christmas celebration : Santa Fe traditions : foods & crafts / Richard P. Clawson ; text by Jann Arrington Wolcott.

      p.   cm.

    ISBN 0-940666-68-5

    1. Christmas cookery.   2. Christmas decorations—New Mexico—Santa Fe.   3. Christmas—New Mexico—Santa Fe—History.   4. Santa Fe (N.M.)—Social life and customs.

    I. Wolcott, Jann Arrington.   II. Title.

TX739.2.C45C49   1995

745.594'12'0978956—dc20   95–32963

                                                             CIP

First Edition

10 9 8 7 6 5 4 3 2 1

Printed in Hong Kong

Acknowledgments

Special thanks go to: John Wolcott, Faye and Walter Oliver, Sharyn Carr, Christina and Mark Church, Richard and Lucy Zeng, Christopher Watt, Eliot Sierra, Nancy Bouchet, Susan Weber, Ed Berry, Ann Miller, Aldo Picchi, David Salk, Marion Goodell, Arny and Judy Katz, Brenda Katz, Matt Saiz, Susan LaPoint, Arlena Markinson, Nedra Matteucci, and Jim and Elizabeth McGordy, Don Strel, and the Santa Fe Ski Area. Thanks also to Harmon Houghton, Marcia Keegan, Sara Held, Ann Mason, SunFlower Elliott, and Michael Ottersen of Clear Light Publishers.

Dedication

This book is dedicated to the memory of my grandmother,
Anna Rose Paddock Laughridge, whom everyone called "Mom."
She loved Christmas and brought it to life for me.
It is also dedicated to Michael Oller, without whose
encouragement and help this book
would not have been possible.

Manger scene, Jemez Pueblo. Each year a different family is given the honor of providing a "home" for the Holy Family from December 24 to January 6. Statues are brought from the church, and a manger scene is created for them. Everyone in the pueblo comes to celebrate and to enjoy a feast. This photograph was taken at the home of Lenore Toledo in 1992. Photograph © by Marcia Keegan.

Contents

Midwinter Celebrations

Customs we now associate with Christmas come from all over the world, and some are far older than one might suppose. As Christianity spread, the celebration of Christmas was enriched by elements of many ancient religious festivals, including those of the Celts, Romans, and Egyptians.

Although the Bible doesn't give a specific date for the birth of Christ, December 25 was officially declared to be Christmas by Pope Julius I in the year A.D. 350. Prior to that, it was celebrated (as it is today by the Greek Orthodox Church) on January 6. Scholars speculate that December 25 was chosen because midwinter celebrations had existed for thousands of years—for example, the Winter Festival of Dionysus in ancient Greece, the Roman Saturnalia, the Jewish Festival of Lights (or Hanukkah), and winter solstice celebrations such as the Celtic Yule. Even the early Egyptians celebrated a midwinter festival, believing that Horus, son of Isis, was born during that time.

Additionally, Mithras, the ancient Persian god of light and truth, was believed to have been born out of a rock on December 25. Mithraism was the state religion of the Roman Empire prior to Christianity, and the festival of Dies Invicti Solis (The Day of the Invincible Sun) was held on Mithras's birthday.

Emperor Constantine I reportedly adhered to Mithraism up to the time of his conversion to Christianity and was instrumental in transforming the major festival of his old religion into the principal feast day of his new faith: the birthday of the sun god became the birthday of the Son of God. It is also interesting to note that Christmas is celebrated between the dates of two ancient Roman festivals, the Saturnalia and the Feast of the Kalends, and clearly retains characteristics of both celebrations.

The Saturnalia predated recorded Roman history and was observed for a week (beginning December 17) to mark a legendary golden age when Saturn, the god of plenty, ruled the world. It was celebrated by feasting, merrymaking, and a general attitude of goodwill. During that week, wars temporarily ceased, gifts were exchanged, and evergreen boughs and berries were brought indoors to decorate homes and dispel the gloom of winter.

The Feast of the Kalends, which followed in early January, marked the beginning of a new year. The old year was ushered out with unrestrained feasting and revelry—much as New Year's is still celebrated today.

As the Christian faith spread into northern Europe, elements of ancient celebrations, such as the Celtic winter solstice celebration of Yule, were preserved in the observance of Christmas. The word *yule* may have derived from the Old German language, and refers to the turning of the seasons or the rising of the wheel of the sun after the winter solstice. Central to these festivities was the lighting of the yule log, symbolizing warmth and light to counter the cold and darkness of winter. The log (often an entire tree

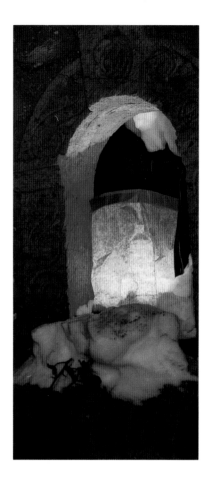

(Opposite page) Image of a Navajo kachina (spirit being) by Leslie Francisco, Navajo medicine man from Crystal, New Mexico, in an old Santa Fe adobe house with a kiva fireplace. Photograph © by Marcia Keegan.

(Above) Farolito (paper lantern) in a stone arch. A farolito consists of a brown paper bag containing a lighted candle held in place with sand. Originally inspired by Chinese lanterns, farolitos became popular in New Mexico in the late 1800s, when manufactured paper bags came into use. Photograph © by Paul De Domenico.

trunk) was blessed by the Druids before being lit with a piece of the previous year's log. Its embers were believed to cure ailments, avert lightning, and bring good luck during the coming year.

In the dead of winter, the idea of rebirth and fertility was tremendously important. The evergreen (a symbol of the life that would return in the spring) was used for ancient Yule decorations, along with holly, ivy, and mistletoe. Mistletoe was considered especially sacred and played an important part in Druid ceremonies. The modern custom of kissing under the mistletoe is probably a holdover from ancient fertility ceremonies.

As Daniel J. Foley states in *Christmas the World Over*, "In adapting some of the practices of all these festivals, the early fathers of the new Christian church captured the spirit of the festival, which was rebirth, and transformed it to signify the coming of Christ; thus, an ancient festival was given a new meaning" (page 14).

Through the centuries, different holiday customs developed and spread from country to country. The custom of the Christmas tree comes most directly from Germany, where Christmas (*Weihnachten*, meaning sacred or holy night) is celebrated with great fervor. But the practice of decorating trees goes back thousands of years and is associated with many cultures. The ancient Egyptians celebrated the winter solstice by adorning their houses and temples with date palm fronds. Both the Druids and the Romans decorated trees in honor of their gods. However, it was in medieval Germany that the custom acquired a Christian context.

In those days in Germany it was customary to celebrate December 24 as the feast day of Adam and Eve, with plays reenacting their fall from the Garden of Eden. A main set piece of these plays was the "paradise tree," an evergreen with apples hanging on it. When the church suppressed such performances, many German households began to set up their own paradise trees on Christmas Eve. Paper flowers, cookies (as a symbol of the Communion wafer), and other fruits were later added as decorations. By the nineteenth century the custom had spread across Europe and to the United States.

St. Nicholas, who was born in Asia Minor around A.D. 280, was considered the patron saint of children, sailors, and unwed women. He was first incorporated into Christmas (*Kertsmisse*) customs by the Dutch, who called him "Santa Niklaus." This name was transformed later into "*Sinter Klass*" and finally "Santa Claus."

The custom of caroling may have spread from Greece, where for centuries children have gone from house to house on Christmas morning singing *kalanda* (carols) telling of the birth of the Christ Child. *Nacimientos*, or manger scenes, probably originated in Spain. And from Mexico we get poinsettias (called "flowers of Christmas Eve"), *piñatas* (earthenware jars shaped like angels, birds, donkeys, or other animals and filled with candy and toys), *luminarias* (bonfires), and the tradition of *Las Posadas* (a Spanish folk drama reenacting Mary and Joseph's search for shelter in Bethlehem).

The masked dance known as *Los Matachines*, which is performed during the month of December in Santa Fe, nearby Spanish villages, and Indian pueblos, was introduced to New Mexico by Spanish conquistadors in the late sixteenth century. The costumes and dance style were probably brought to Spain in the eighth century by the Moors.

However its customs have evolved over the millennia, and no matter whether it is called *Navidad*, *Noël*, *Weihnachten*, or *Kertsmisse*, Christmas is the most lavishly celebrated holiday in the Christian world. And nowhere is it celebrated with more diversity and spirit than in Santa Fe, the City of the Holy Faith.

Snow-covered Pueblo-style ladder leaning against an adobe building. These sturdy wooden ladders have been adopted by many Santa Fe residents as a decorative architectural feature. Photograph © by Don Strel.

Christmas Comes to Santa Fe

Santa Fe. For centuries the name has evoked an aura of adventure and romance. As the oldest capital city in the United States, it has served as a seat of government for Spain, Mexico, the Confederacy, and the United States.

Christmas in Santa Fe is unlike Christmas anywhere else in the world. The ancient city celebrates the holiday season with a blending of colorful traditions from the Native American, Spanish, and Anglo cultures that have coexisted in northern New Mexico for hundreds of years.

The birth of Christ was first celebrated in Santa Fe in 1610 by Spanish colonists who had braved the treacherous months-long trek north from Mexico City. Led by Don Pedro de Peralta, the hardy group established the first permanent Spanish settlement (two other settlements a few miles to the north had previously been abandoned) on the ruins of a prehistoric Indian pueblo that nestled against the base of a spectacular mountain range. The settlers named the snow-topped mountains the Sangre de Cristos (Blood of Christ) because of their crimson hue when bathed by the setting sun. Their village was christened La Villa Real de la Santa Fe de San Francisco, The Royal City of the Holy Faith of St. Francis. It marked the end of the one-thousand-mile Camino Real (Royal Road) from Mexico City.

The Spaniards, travel-weary and far from home, settled in the beautiful but inhospitable land. It was not an easy life. The colonists persevered, equipped with a few treasured farming tools and household items; the sheep, goats, cattle, and horses that had survived the arduous journey; and their unshakable Roman Catholic faith.

These colonists had been preceded to the remote high-desert country of northern New Mexico by Francisco Vásquez de Coronado in 1540 and later by Spanish conquistadors in search of Cíbola, a province supposedly containing seven cities of gold and silver. Although the conquistadors never found the Seven Cities of Cíbola, they discovered vast, majestic landscapes and multistoried communities inhabited by a peaceful, agricultural people. To the great disappointment of the Spaniards, the buildings were constructed of adobe (sun-dried mud bricks)

(Opposite page) Coyote fence on Canyon Road. Coyote fences, which were originally used by Indians and ranchers to protect livestock, are constructed usually of rough cedar poles and have become popular in Santa Fe. Photograph © by Marcia Keegan.

(Above) Wood vendor's burro wagon on Palace Avenue at the plaza, Santa Fe, New Mexico, December, 1918. Photograph by Wesley Bradfield. Courtesy Museum of New Mexico (neg. no. 12986).

and stone rather than precious metals. They called the communities *pueblos* (towns), and their residents became known as Pueblo Indians.

Although to Spanish eyes it lacked material wealth, the Native American culture was rich in tradition, spirituality, and ceremony. For thousands of years the Indians had lived in harmony with nature. Their religion, based on a reverence for Mother Earth and Father Sky, perceived all things as living, and celebrated a sense of unity with the environment, other species, and all aspects of creation.

As the number of Spanish settlers in northern New Mexico grew, so did their control over the lives of the indigenous people. Fueled by religious fervor, Spanish missionaries worked to eradicate the Native American religion and to replace it with Christianity. To this end, they built mission churches within the pueblos, discouraged traditional Indian dances and *kiva* (ceremonial lodge) rituals, and insisted on the observation of Christian rites and holidays.

The Indians were also given Spanish surnames, and their ancient pueblos were renamed after Catholic saints. For example, the Tewa village of Powoghe (meaning "Place Where the Waters Meet") became San Ildefonso. Other nearby pueblos whose Spanish saints' names are commonly used today are San Juan, Santa Clara, San Felipe, and Santo Domingo.

After eighty-two years of Spanish rule, the traditionally peaceful Pueblo Indians revolted. Led by a San Juan Indian named Popé, they united in the Pueblo Revolt of 1680 and captured Santa Fe. The surviving Spaniards fled south to what is now El Paso, Texas, and for thirteen years Santa Fe was occupied by the victorious Indians.

In 1693, General Don Diego de Vargas and some eight hundred colonists reconquered the city, and for the next 128 years Santa Fe served as the capital of Spain's northernmost New World province. Gradually, the Indians adopted Christianity, incorporating it into their own beliefs and traditions. For example, Christmas

(Opposite page) The soft glow of farolitos (paper bag lanterns) lights up Christmas Eve celebrations in New Mexico. Photograph © by Eduardo Fuss.

(Left) Christmas tree, Palace of the Governors, Santa Fe, New Mexico, 1956. Courtesy Museum of New Mexico (neg. no. 1642).

Mass was celebrated at the pueblos followed by ancient winter solstice dances meant to ensure hunting success and to honor the spirits of the deer, antelope, buffalo, and other animals upon which the Indians' survival depended.

New Mexico's cultural isolation came to an end in 1821 when Mexican revolutionists overthrew Spanish colonial rule and Santa Fe became the capital of the northern province of the Republic of Mexico. The territory was, for the first time, open to trade with Americans. Santa Fe became the last stop on the famed Santa Fe Trail. The result was an influx of *extranjeros* (foreigners), including mountain men, fur trappers, and merchants of various nationalities. Five years later the United States declared war on Mexico. On August 18, 1846, U. S. Army General Stephen Watts Kearny raised the American flag over the Palace of the Governors, and Santa Fe was on its way to becoming the tricultural city that it is today.

It was not until the arrival of the Atchison, Topeka and Santa Fe Railway in 1880, however, that Santa Fe strongly felt the influence of the Anglo culture and was introduced to new Christmas traditions such as decorated trees, Santa Claus, stuffed turkey, and eggnog. The result, more than a century later, is a beautifully bizarre, harmonious yuletide celebration of cultural diversity that is unique to Santa Fe.

Three Traditions of Christmas

The Christmas season has come to mean weeks of shopping and a whirl of holiday activities for most Santa Feans. But that wasn't always the case. In years past, Christmas in northern New Mexico was a simple religious celebration centered around performances of *Las Posadas*, Midnight Mass on Christmas Eve, and Pueblo Indian dances. The festivities always included a traditional feast of *posole, enchiladas, tamales, carne adovada, sopaipillas, empanaditas,* and *bizcochitos,* the traditional anise-flavored Christmas cookies.

In the following interviews, four members of old New Mexico families, representing the state's three main cultures, share their earliest memories of Christmas. They also provide special recipes traditionally associated with the holidays.

Adam and Santana Martinez

Adam Martinez, a full-blooded Tewa Indian, was born at San Ildefonso Pueblo in 1903, the eldest son of famed potters Julian and Maria Martinez. A handsome man with high cheekbones and long grey braids, Adam's quiet dignity is balanced by a quick wit and a mischievous sense of humor.

Adam has lived at the pueblo all of his life, except for the years he attended the Santa Fe Indian School. His people have been in this area for more than a thousand years, living in cliff dwellings at nearby Tsankawi (now part of Bandelier National Monument) and two other nearby areas before moving to the Rio Grande Valley during the early 1500s. Since that time, they have farmed the fertile land beside the Rio Grande that is known in Tewa as Powoghe, but was renamed San Ildefonso by early Spanish settlers. Nearby looms Black Mesa, called Tunyo by the Tewas and long revered as a sacred site.

Adam's mother, the late Maria Martinez, is perhaps the best known of all Pueblo Indian potters. She brought fame to San Ildefonso Pueblo in the early 1920s when, inspired by potsherds unearthed at archaeological digs, she developed her distinctive matte-on-black pottery. Maria's pottery was decorated by her husband, Julian, a talented painter whose paintings and graphics hang in major American museums.

Adam, now retired from farming his ancestral land and serving his pueblo in the role of elder advisor, inherited the artistic abilities of his parents. He still creates exquisite black pottery pieces, including graceful bear fetishes. He is also known for his musical talent. Adam's voice is strong and clear as, at the age of ninety-one, he drums and sings ancient Tewa songs for visitors on the sun-washed portal of his modest pueblo home.

Santana Roybal Martinez, Adam's wife for almost seventy years, was also born and raised at the pueblo. Santana is a member of another artistic family. Her late uncle, Crecencio, and brother, Awa Tsireh, were both accomplished painters; and her aunt, Tonita Martinez Roybal, was another well-known San Ildefonso potter.

(Opposite page) Matachines Dance, San Ildefonso Pueblo, December 25, 1950. Photograph by John L. Champe. Courtesy Museum of New Mexico (neg. no. 49316).

Santana's natural creativity was encouraged and further developed by Maria and Julian after she joined their family. After Julian's death in 1943, Santana worked closely with her mother-in-law, decorating Maria's pottery. Today, Santana is a nationally acclaimed artist in her own right, collaborating on pottery pieces with Adam. Although the couple now prefers to stay close to home, they still occasionally travel to other states to teach pottery workshops.

Santana, the soft-spoken matriarch of the extensive Martinez clan, joined her husband on the portal to share memories of Christmas at San Ildefonso Pueblo.

"The Spaniards came to this land and taught us about their Catholic God," Adam said. "So now we are Christians. But before that time we had our own ceremonies and dances. Our Indian ways still come first because they are part of our older religion."

Santana nodded her agreement. "We Indians celebrate Christmas in our own way," she said, "honoring both the Christian and our ancient traditions." She went on to say that her earliest memories of Christmas center on food preparation. "There was always a lot of cooking

going on here at the pueblo on Christmas Eve," she said, "starting early in the morning. The main dishes were red and green chile and *posole*, made with pork, chile, and corn. My mother also made *sopa* (a bread pudding made with cheese, raisins, cinnamon, and sugar), and she baked bread, pies, and *bizcochitos* outside in the *horno*, the outdoor oven. I remember my father making many trips to gather wood so that we would have enough for the holidays."

Adam listed pies and *bizcochitos* as his favorite Christmas foods. "Oh, and chile," he added with a grin. "I always eat a lot of chile. It's very good for you."

Christmas traditions at San Ildefonso, as at the other New Mexico pueblos, reflect an interesting commingling of diverse cultures. Christmas Mass is followed by four days of ceremonial dancing. The animal dances—Buffalo, Deer, and Eagle—are an integral part of a Pueblo Christmas. Holdovers from ancient winter solstice celebrations, the dances are a Native American form of prayer, performed to honor the animals and to acknowledge their revered place in nature.

An especially interesting Christmas Day dance performed at Spanish villages and the pueblos near Santa Fe is *Los Matachines*, an exotic, masked dance performed to sixteenth-century Spanish folk music. It probably originated with the Moors in Spain and was brought to the pueblos by Spanish colonists.

"It wouldn't seem like Christmas without the dances," Santana said, "especially *Los Matachines*." She went on to explain that practice begins in early December. Years ago, the dances would continue into the night, with the performers going from house to house. "Everyone would give them presents like bread or pies," she said. "But that's all changed. It's one of the customs we've lost."

Both Adam and Santana used to participate in the Christmas dances, and Adam played the drum on ceremonial days. Now he limits his

(Far left) Adam Martinez, son of potters Maria and Julian Martinez, is a lifelong resident and elder advisor of San Ildefonso Pueblo. Photograph © by Jane Mont and Chris Mitchell.

(Top left) Adam and Santana Martinez on their wedding day, November 3, 1926, San Ildefonso Pueblo. Photograph courtesy of Adam and Santana Martinez.

(Bottom left) Adam and Santana Martinez, June 1990, San Ildefonso Pueblo. Photograph © by Jane Mont and Chris Mitchell.

drumming and singing to private gatherings of family and friends.

"In the old days we could have Midnight Mass only every three years," Santana explained, "because we had to share a priest with Santa Clara and Tesuque pueblos. He would come from Santa Cruz in a wagon on Christmas Eve and, if he said the last Mass here at San Ildefonso, he would stay overnight.

"We would all stay up late, even if we didn't have Midnight Mass. At midnight, the church bells would ring and ring, telling the people that the Christ Child was born. Everyone in the pueblo would then go to the church. We would pray and leave a present—like a loaf of bread or a fruit pie—as a gift for the baby Jesus. Afterwards my grandmother would have coffee and something special fixed for us to eat." Santana paused, her expression wistful at the memory. "It was always very late when we got to bed on Christmas Eve!"

Christmas trees were not a custom in Indian homes when Santana and Adam were young. Santana recalled the first time she helped to decorate a tree, as a young student at the Pueblo Day School. "The Anglo teacher sent some of the boys out to the hills to cut a small piñon tree. Then we decorated it with colored paper rings and strings of popcorn. We were very excited when the teacher gave us gifts of candy, nuts, oranges, and cookies.

"Later, I think it was in the 1930s, we started giving presents to each other. We'd have a Christmas program at the school on Christmas Eve. Everyone from the pueblo would go and take little gifts to exchange."

At San Ildefonso Pueblo, Christmas revolves around family, friends, and the church. In addition to other gifts, there are stockings filled with candy, nuts, and perhaps an orange for the children to find on Christmas morning. "We don't go out," Santana said. "We celebrate quietly with our family and friends—and with lots of food."

"I remember one special Christmas," Adam

interjected. "Our oldest son, Frank, was small, and he wanted a saddle. So I bought one for him and had a friend dressed like Santa Claus bring it into the house strapped to his back. All the children were so excited by that." Adam and Santana both smiled at the memory. "Yes," Adam said, "Christmas has always been a happy time."

Deer Dance at San Ildefonso Pueblo, January 23, 1920. Photograph by Wesley Bradfield. Courtesy Museum of New Mexico (neg. no. 90120).

Pueblo Indian Christmas Recipes

GREEN CHILE STEW

2 pounds meat (pork, beef, mutton, venison, rabbit, or chicken), diced

2 tablespoons lard or oil

3 cups water (or meat stock, if available)

6 ounces green chile, diced

1 large onion, diced

2 squashes, diced

3 large potatoes, diced

6 tomatoes

1 cup corn

Brown the meat in the lard or oil. Then add the water or stock and bring it to a boil. Lower the temperature and cook, covered, for several hours until the meat is tender. Add the vegetables and simmer for approximately 45 more minutes. Serves 6 to 8.

PUEBLO LAMB STEW

1 tablespoon flour

1½ teaspoons salt

2 teaspoons ground red chile

2 pounds stewing lamb, cubed

2 tablespoons lard or oil

6 small onions, chopped

3 sweet green peppers, chopped

5 cups corn kernels

1 cup stewed tomatoes

5 dried juniper berries, crushed

4 cups lamb stock (or water)

Combine seasonings and flour. Dredge the meat lightly. In a large saucepan brown the meat in lard or oil. Transfer the meat to a plate. Sauté onions and peppers until slightly wilted. Add the corn. Return the meat to the pan and add the remaining ingredients. Simmer, covered, for 2 hours, or until the meat is tender, stirring occasionally. Serves 4 to 6.

ATOLE

1 cup blue cornmeal

3 cups water

2 tablespoons lard

Dash of salt

Dissolve the cornmeal in 1 cup water. Bring 2 cups of water to a boil in a large pot. Add the lard and salt. Slowly add the cornmeal, stirring until the mixture is a thick consistency. Serve with honey or sprinkled with sugar. Serves 4.

RABBIT IN ATOLE

1 rabbit, cut into serving pieces

4 tablespoons lard

1 large onion, diced

4–5 tablespoons ground red chile

Dash of salt

⅔ cup blue cornmeal

Using a deep skillet, brown the rabbit in the lard. Add the onion, chile, and salt and simmer until the onion is soft. Add enough water to cover the rabbit completely. Put a lid on the skillet and simmer for 2 hours. Before serving, slowly add the cornmeal, stirring until it thickens. Serves 4.

PUEBLO BREAD
(Traditionally baked in a horno, an adobe oven)

2 packages dry yeast

2½ cups warm water

5 tablespoons lard or oil, melted

2 teaspoons salt

9 cups flour

In a large bowl, mix the yeast in ½ cup warm water. Stir in the melted lard or oil and add the salt. Slowly add the flour, while mixing in the remaining 2 cups of water.

Mix and knead the mixture until smooth and elastic. Place the ball of dough in a large oiled bowl and cover with a damp cloth. Let it rise for several hours, until double in bulk. Punch down and knead well. Divide into 4 balls; then place them in 4 oiled round pans. Allow the dough to rise again. Bake for 50 to 60 minutes in a 400-degree oven until the tops of the loaves are golden brown. Makes 4 loaves.

SANTANA'S SOPA (Bread Pudding)

2 eggs, beaten

1 cup raisins

2 teaspoons vanilla

2 teaspoons cinnamon

1 teaspoon cooking oil

1 loaf white bread, toasted

1 cup grated cheddar cheese

½ cup sugar

3 cups hot water

Mix the eggs, raisins, vanilla, and cinnamon and set aside. Spread the cooking oil on all sides of a deep-sided 8 x 10-inch baking pan. Crumb the bread and put ½ the loaf into the baking pan.

Sprinkle ½ of the cheese on top of the bread. Add ½ of the vanilla, raisin, cinnamon, and egg mixture. Repeat the process. Brown the sugar in a saucepan. Add the water slowly, stirring until all the lumps are gone. Pour over the ingredients in the baking pan and bake in a 350-degree oven for 30 minutes or until all the liquid has been absorbed and the pudding is set. Serves 6 to 8.

Concha Ortiz y Pino de Kleven

Concha Ortiz y Pino de Kleven has had a lifelong commitment to preserving New Mexico's Spanish heritage and to the improvement of life for the poor and the handicapped.

Dedication to public service has long been part of Concha's family heritage. She is a descendant of Spanish colonial families from Castile and Aragon that settled in northern New Mexico in the sixteenth century. Her great-great-grandfather, Don Pedro Bautista Pino, was a delegate to Spain's Parliament from the "New World north of Mexico" in 1812 and signed the first Constitution of Spain ensuring freedom of speech in the Latin American world.

Concha's determination to improve the quality of life for all New Mexicans is apparent in the long and diverse list of her accomplishments. After graduating from the University of New Mexico, she held key positions in the New Mexico Legislature, including state representative for three terms, starting in 1937. She was the first woman in the United States to be elected majority whip in a state legislature. During her political career, she fought for women's right to serve on juries, sponsored legislation that founded the School of Inter-American Affairs at the University of New Mexico, and introduced a bill requiring the teaching of Spanish to all of New Mexico's elementary schoolchildren. In addition, she founded a school for traditional Spanish colonial arts and crafts and served as both dean of women and professor of history and culture at the University of Albuquerque.

In recent years, Concha has been involved in volunteer work on national, state, and local levels. The many contributions of this extraordinary New Mexican have earned her the unofficial title of the "Grande Dame of Santa Fe."

"When I was a child, Christmas had a more reverent feeling than it does now," said Concha. "It was a religious celebration, a season of hu-

(Opposite page) Concha Ortiz y Pino de Kleven is a descendant of Spanish colonists whose long and varied career in public service reflects her love of her home state. Photograph © by Marcia Keegan.

(Left) Concha Ortiz y Pino de Kleven at her family's Galisteo ranch, Christmas, 1914. Photograph courtesy of Concha Ortiz y Pino de Kleven.

manitarianism, generosity, friendship, helpfulness, and sharing." She smiled, remembering. "Christmas was also a time of the most delicious smells in my grandmother's home."

Concha was born in Galisteo, a small sheep ranching village twenty miles southeast of Santa Fe, on May 20, 1910. She spent the first nine years of her life in the spacious hacienda of her grandmother, Doña Josefa Ortiz de Davis, before moving to her parents' home in Santa Fe.

"I remember the excitement, the unity, and the cooperation of the whole Galisteo community at Christmas," Concha reminisced. "The holiday season really started on December 12, with *La Fiesta de Nuestra Señora de Guadalupe*, the reenactment of Mary's appearance to an Indian peasant boy in Mexico City. That was the beginning of the Christmas activity and the extensive food preparation. First, there was the communal butchering of a calf, some lambs, and a hog. Then the meat was roasted in *hornos*, outdoor beehive-shaped clay ovens. It was hard work. The *hornos* had to be stoked with wood, and the food had to be constantly watched."

Concha elaborated on the traditional pre-holiday preparation: "Women from the village would gather in my grandmother's large kitchen to make blue corn *tortillas* and *buñuelos* (deep-fried bread), *tamales, adobo* (pork cooked with red chile, oregano, and garlic), *pastelitos* (little pies made with dried fruit), and *empanaditas* (fried pastries filled with ground meat, piñon nuts, spices, and wine). I remember sitting in the kitchen sampling all the wonderful dishes as they were prepared."

Posole has long been a traditional New Mexico Christmas dish. Concha recalled large pots of the pork and hominy stew hanging from a metal tripod in the fireplace in her grandmother's bedroom. "The fire was continually tended," she said, "so the *posole* cooked all night long. My, how delicious it smelled when we awoke the next morning!

"After the Christmas feast had been prepared, Doña Josefa would distribute the food to all of the villagers, keeping only enough for our family and the people who lived with us," Concha explained. "There were a lot of very poor people in our village, but no one went hungry or without love during Christmas."

In spite of all the excitement and food preparation, the religious aspect of Christmas was always emphasized. *"Las Posadas,* the reenactment of Mary and Joseph's search for shelter, was a very important part of Christmas to all of us in Galisteo," Concha said. "The folk drama began nine days before Christmas when a young lady was chosen from the village to play the Virgin Mary, along with an older gentleman to play St. Joseph. Lucifer was always played by an athletic young man dressed in a red uniform and carrying a long pitchfork.

"Every evening for nine days the Blessed Mother, riding on a burro, would be led by St. Joseph to a different home, asking for admittance. They would sing the lyrics that everyone in the village knew by heart. Lucifer and the people inside the homes would then sing the answering lyrics, replying that there was no room in that inn, and telling them to go away. Lucifer would also have a good time with the village children, warning them to behave or they wouldn't get a gift when the child Jesus came.

"All the villagers marched in procession, past the *luminarias,* which lit the way for Mary and Joseph as they went to the nine different homes. The evening would end with everyone being invited into a host's home for refreshments and to sing old Spanish carols, such as *'Noche de Paz'* and *'Vamos Todos a Belen,'* accompanied by guitars and violins. It was a wonderful tradition. *Las Posadas* was truly the essence of the religious aspect of Christmas for us in those days."

There was rarely a priest in residence in Galisteo during Concha's youth. "When a priest was able to travel from Santa Fe or Pecos on *La Noche Buena,* Christmas Eve, we would have a Midnight Mass, which was called *La Misa del Gallo,* the Mass of the Rooster," Concha said. "If a priest couldn't come, the villagers would gather at the church to pray and sing Christmas songs."

Christmas trees, an Anglo tradition that came later, were not part of the celebrations in Spanish villages during those early days. Concha explained that holiday decorations in Galisteo typically consisted of handmade paper flowers and piñon branches placed around *nacimientos,* manger scenes made of wood, straw, or ceramic.

"On Christmas Eve and Christmas Day the church bells in the village would ring for hours," she continued. "It was a day of play, of romping and singing and dancing. And of visiting with friends. It wasn't until later, when we became more American, that we started buying and wrapping presents. We might receive one present. Christmas didn't involve the feverish shopping that it does now."

From the age of nine, when she was enrolled in the Loretto Academy for Girls, a Catholic girls' school, Concha spent Christmas at her family home in Santa Fe. "The Spanish so-

Los Pastores *(The Shepherds), a traditional Spanish miracle play, performed at St. Francis Auditorium, Santa Fe, New Mexico, January, 1920. Photograph by Wesley Bradfield. Courtesy Museum of New Mexico (neg. no. 13692).*

Traditional Spanish Christmas Recipes

RED CHILE SAUCE

This is the basic red chile sauce that is used in *posole*, *carne adovada* (also called *adobo*), and *enchiladas*. The intensity of heat and the taste will depend on the kind of chiles used. New Mexico red or Anaheim chiles are recommended, but the sauce can be made with any moderately hot dried red chile.

1 dozen dried red chiles
2 cups chicken stock
1 tablespoon oregano
Garlic powder and salt to taste

Steam the chiles until they plump up. Remove the seeds and skins and run the chiles through a blender or food processor. Then put them through a colander to remove any remaining seeds or skin, until velvety smooth. Add the chicken stock, oregano, and garlic powder and salt to taste. Makes 3 cups.

POSOLE

1 large, lean boneless pork roast
4 cups chicken stock
1 large onion, chopped
1 clove garlic, mashed
2 tablespoons oregano
6 cups hominy (or prepared chicos, *if available)*
1 cup Red Chile Sauce (see recipe above)

Simmer the pork roast in the chicken stock for 6 to 8 hours, or until the meat shreds easily with a fork. Remove any fat and gristle and spoon the fat from the top of the cooking liquid. Add the onion, garlic, oregano, hominy, and chile sauce. If the sauce is too thick, add water to achieve the desired consistency. Simmer for an additional 2 hours. Serves 6.

ciety here was very formal and closely knit in those days," she said. "My parents would have a big party before Midnight Mass. Even the priest would attend. Then after Mass we'd come back and eat some more before going to bed.

"On Christmas morning, it was the custom in those days for little children to go from door to door, saying, '*Mis Christmas, mis Christmas,*' 'My Christmas, my Christmas.' My mother always had paper bags—many, many of them—filled with candies, oranges, and other gifts for the little visitors.

"The Christmases of my youth, in both Galisteo and Santa Fe, were centered around religion," Concha concluded. "There was no hatred at that time of year because everyone was so imbued with the spirit of love. In those days, gifts came from the Christ Child not from Santa Claus. We exchanged gifts of food, but the real Christmas gifts were friendship and true brotherly love."

ENCHILADAS

12 corn tortillas

⅓ cup vegetable oil (traditionally, lard was used)

3–4 cups Red Chile Sauce (page 25)

3 cups cooked ground beef or shredded chicken
   (optional)

3 cups longhorn cheese, grated

2 small onions, minced

4 eggs (optional)

Fry the tortillas in the oil until soft and drain on paper towels. Heat the chile sauce. Stack 3 tortillas on each plate and top with meat, cheese, onions, and sauce. Fry the eggs in the remaining oil. Top each *enchilada* stack with a fried egg. Serves 4.

CARNE ADOVADA (ADOBO)

2–3 cups Red Chile Sauce (page 25)

10 lean pork chops, pork steaks, or 1½
   pounds cubed pork roast

Pour the sauce over the pork in a large bowl and marinate for 24 hours. Bake the pork and sauce in a baking dish at 350 degrees for 2 hours. Serves 6.

A contemporary reenactment of Los Pastores *(The Shepherds). Photograph © by Eduardo Fuss.*

BUÑUELOS

This is a chewy, deep-fried bread with ancient origins. A staple of shepherds in the Middle East because it's quick to prepare and keeps well, the recipe was probably brought to New Mexico by way of Spain and Morocco. (A more elegant cousin, the *sopaipilla*, is rolled out thin before cooking so it puffs up.)

3 cups flour, sifted

1 teaspoon salt

3 teaspoons baking powder (not used in early recipes)

1 pound lard

Sift together the flour, salt, and baking powder. Work in about ¼ cup lard. Add enough water to make the dough moist and pliable. Mix well. Pat into large pancakes and punch a hole in the middle of each. Deep-fry in hot lard. Makes 36.

SOPAIPILLAS

2 cups flour

1 teaspoon salt

2 teaspoons baking powder

2 tablespoons lard or vegetable shortening

½ cup lukewarm water

Mix all the dry ingredients together well. Cut in the lard or shortening. Add the lukewarm water to make a soft dough. Roll on a lightly floured board to about ¼ inch thick. Cut into 4-inch squares and fry in hot lard (or vegetable shortening) until golden brown on both sides, turning once. Drain and serve warm with honey or butter. Makes 24.

FLAN (Baked Custard)

1½ cups granulated sugar

3 egg whites

8 egg yolks

2 13-ounce cans evaporated milk

2 teaspoons vanilla

Pour 1 cup of the granulated sugar into a loaf pan. Place over medium heat and melt the sugar, stirring constantly with a wooden spoon. When the sugar is golden brown, remove it from the heat and tilt the pan so that the caramel coats the inside of the pan evenly. Set aside to cool.

Beat the egg whites and yolks with the remaining sugar, evaporated milk, and vanilla. Pour the mixture into the caramel-coated pan. Cover the pan with foil. Place the pan in a larger pan containing about an inch of hot water.

Bake at least 1 hour at 350 degrees (or until a knife inserted in the middle of the custard comes out clean). Refrigerate at least 2 hours—preferably overnight. Before serving, run a knife around the edge of the pan and turn the custard out onto a small platter. Serves 8 to 10.

BIZCOCHITOS
(Traditional Christmas Cookies)

1 pound lard

1 cup sugar

2 eggs

2 teaspoons aniseed

6 cups flour

3 teaspoons baking powder

1 teaspoon salt

½ cup sugar and 1 teaspoon cinnamon, mixed well

Mix the lard and sugar until creamy. Add the eggs and aniseed and cream some more. Sift the flour, baking powder, and salt and mix with the first mixture. Add enough water to hold the dough together. Roll out the dough ¼ inch thick on a floured board and cut into Christmas shapes with cookie cutters or a knife. Sprinkle with the sugar and cinnamon mixture and bake in a 375-degree oven for 10 to 12 minutes. Makes 6 dozen.

House on Canyon. This historic street is filled with shops, galleries, and artists' studios. Photograph © by Marcia Keegan.

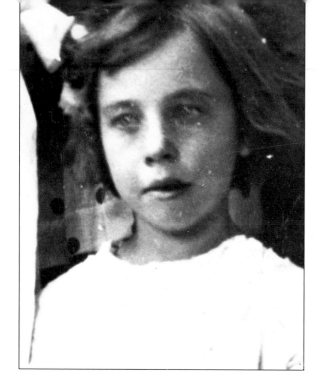

Ada Nowlin Pick

A member of one of New Mexico's pioneering families, Ada Nowlin Pick was born on a cattle ranch north of Santa Fe in 1910. Her parents, John and Mattie Nowlin, were Irish Protestant homesteaders who came west from Missouri in a covered wagon. Ada attended public school for the first time in the seventh grade; prior to that time she had been taught at home by her schoolteacher mother.

"I had a beautiful childhood," she said. "Mother would teach me for about three hours a day. The rest of the time I rode my pony, picked wildflowers, and helped in the kitchen, making biscuits and bread."

Ada left the ranch to attend the Loretto Academy for Girls in Santa Fe in her early teens. She graduated in 1928 and went on to attend Highlands University, the University of New Mexico, and Columbia University, majoring in education.

Ada taught school, both in Santa Fe and in outlying rural districts, for several years. In 1935 she married Leo Pick, a merchant who had immigrated to America from Austria at the age of fourteen. He later came to northern Mexico to join his brothers, Henry and Emil, who were successful merchants. "My late husband

used to joke that they sold everything 'from cookies to coffins' in their local general stores," Ada said.

The Picks had two daughters, Patricia and Margaret, and lived in Santa Fe for almost fifty years, just blocks from the plaza. A dedicated educator who authored several children's books and served as education commissioner for New Mexico for eight years, Ada shared her memories of Christmas in Santa Fe more than half a century ago.

"Christmas was a much simpler affair in my childhood," she said. "It wasn't as elaborate or commercialized as it is now. When I was growing up on our family ranch, we made almost all of the gifts that we exchanged. You know, in those days, it didn't take much to make us happy. For example, certain fruits were hard to come by in this area. To find an orange or banana in your stocking on Christmas morning was a real thrill!"

Ada went on to describe the holiday barn dances traditionally held during the Christmas season with the other ranching families in the area. "Everyone would bring food," she said. "There would be tables laden with ham, turkey, and venison. Vegetable dishes consisted of whatever had been 'put up,' pickled, or preserved in jars from gardens the summer before. And the desserts! I'll never forget all of the delicious fruit cobblers and pies.

"Some of the ranch hands would play the fiddle and guitar, and everyone would dance until dawn. We children stayed awake as long as we could. Our parents would wake us up for a big country breakfast—pancakes, ham and eggs, biscuits and gravy—the next morning, before the party finally broke up. People worked so hard in those days. They rarely took the time to socialize like they do now. So when the occasion to celebrate arose during the holidays, everyone made the most of it. Those old-time barn dances were memorable occasions!"

About a week before Christmas, the Nowlins would go into the mountains to cut their own

(Left) Ada Nowlin, age five. Photograph courtesy of Ada Nowlin Pick.

(Above) Ada Nowlin Pick, lifelong resident of Santa Fe and daughter of Irish Protestant homesteaders. Photograph © by Jane Mont and Chris Mitchell.

tree. "That was such fun," Ada said. "It was a real family occasion. We'd take a big picnic lunch and make a day of it. After we got home, we children would make ornaments for the tree out of whatever was available—things like tin cans, colored paper, and pinecones. We'd also string popcorn and cranberries. We had the most wonderful times decorating the Christmas tree!"

Ada further reminisced about the days when Santa Fe was "little more than a village" and Christmas centered around church, family, and neighbors.

"When I was a young wife and mother, the community was quite small," she said. "It was also very close-knit. Everyone knew just about everything about everyone else. Especially during the holidays, there was a wonderful feeling of fellowship and goodwill.

"The religious aspect of Christmas used to be much stronger than it is now," Ada continued. "The emphasis was on the birth of Christ, rather than on the arrival of Santa Claus. That was especially true in the educational system, where more religion was brought into school Christmas programs than would be allowed today. We always had great Christmas pageants. That was important because the only Christmas presents many children received in those days were the ones given to them at school."

Ada said that one of the highlights of the Christmas season was always *Las Posadas*, the reenactment of Mary and Joseph's search for shelter in Bethlehem before the birth of Jesus. "Regardless of the weather, there was always a big turnout for the pageant, which lasted for nine evenings," she said. "In fact, snow just added to the drama of the production. *Las Posadas* is still performed on the plaza before Christmas, but now it's an abbreviated version, presented in one evening, instead of the traditional nine. I've always found *Las Posadas* to be a beautiful, moving experience. It's a lovely reminder of what Christmas is all about."

Midnight Mass at St. Francis Cathedral has long been a Christmas tradition in Santa Fe. "Everyone used to attend," Ada said, "even people who weren't Catholic. I'll always remember walking through the snowy winter night to the cathedral, with the church bells ringing, *farolitos* glowing around the plaza, and the air perfumed with piñon burning in fireplaces."

After Midnight Mass, people would gather with friends and relatives for an early Christmas feast. "The menu always included a big kettle of *posole*," Ada said. "*Posole* has been a traditional Santa Fe Christmas Eve dish for as long as I can remember, in Anglo as well as in Spanish and Indian homes."

Ada recalled another Santa Fe tradition, one that she regrets has disappeared. "Early on Christmas morning little children would come around and knock on the door, saying, 'Merry Christmas, Merry Christmas,'" she said. "It was part of that wonderful feeling of community spirit. We always had little presents for them—just like at Halloween!"

After a Christmas dinner that included turkey with all the trimmings—cranberry sauce, piñon corn bread dressing, sweet potatoes, corn, and homemade bread—the Picks would get together with friends and neighbors for a cup of eggnog and some holiday cheer.

Ada especially loved the old Christmas custom of exchanging special foods with friends

The children, Christmas tree and family group at the Henry Schmidt residence after Christmas. Chloride, New Mexico 1894. Photograph by Henry A. Schmidt. Courtesy Museum of New Mexico (neg. no. 58548).

and neighbors. "It was a token of goodwill," she said, "a more personal gesture than exchanging Christmas cards the way people do now. We usually gave gifts of fruitcake or fudge. Our Spanish friends would bring us *bizcochitos* and *empanaditas.*"

Although Santa Fe has grown and changed throughout the years, Ada still finds it a "magical" place to live. "It's beautiful," she said, "any time of the year. But there's something so special about Santa Fe during the Christmas season. I wouldn't want to be anywhere else."

Authentic Frontier Christmas Recipes

SOURDOUGH BREAD STARTER

This recipe was a staple on cattle drives and in frontier kitchens. It was the basis for bread, biscuits, and pancakes. Because yeast wasn't readily available, early cooks substituted soured "potato water," water in which potatoes had been boiled. After several days the water would sour and act as a rising agent.

Add 2½ cups sour potato water to 2 cups flour.

Note: If using yeast rather than potato water, sprinkle 1 package of yeast over the flour; then add 2½ cups of lukewarm water. Put the mixture in a crock jar and store in a warm (but not hot) place to ferment.

SOURDOUGH BISCUITS

½ cup Sourdough Bread Starter (see recipe above)
1 cup milk
2½ cups flour
1 tablespoon sugar
¾ teaspoon salt
2 teaspoons baking powder
⅓ cup shortening
½ teaspoon baking soda

Mix the ½ cup starter with 1 cup milk and 1 cup flour. Let set overnight (or 6 to 8 hours) in a warm place to rise.

Sift together the remaining 1½ cups flour and the other dry ingredients, except the baking soda. Work in the shortening with your fingers or a fork. Dissolve the soda in a little warm water and add it to the starter. Then add the starter to the dry ingredients and mix to make a soft dough. Knead the dough lightly and roll it out to ½ inch thickness. Cut the dough into biscuit shapes. Place the biscuits close together in a well-greased pan, turning them to grease the tops. Cover with a cloth and set in a warm place to rise for 45 minutes. Bake at 375 degrees for 30 to 35 minutes. Makes 1 dozen.

CHRISTMAS MORNING SOURDOUGH PANCAKES

2 eggs
1 cup milk
2 cups Sourdough Bread Starter (page 30)
1½ cups flour
1 teaspoon baking soda
2 teaspoons baking powder
1 teaspoon salt
4 teaspoons sugar

Beat the eggs and add the milk and starter. Sift the flour and other dry ingredients together. Add to the liquid mixture only when you are ready to cook. The batter rises quickly and falls if allowed to stand. Cook the pancakes on a very hot griddle. Serves 4 to 6.

CHRISTMAS MORNING PAN-FRIED QUAIL (OR DOVES)

10–12 quail (or doves)
Salt and pepper
1 pound bacon

Wash the cleaned birds and season them with salt and pepper. Fry the bacon in a large skillet over medium heat until crispy. Remove the bacon from the pan, but keep it in a warm place. Fry the birds in the bacon grease 4 to 5 minutes, turning them continuously to cook them evenly and prevent burning. Remove them from the pan, drain on paper towels, and serve immediately with the bacon. Serves 6.

Pioneer wagon, New Mexico, circa 1920. Photograph by T. Harmon Parkhurst. Courtesy Museum of New Mexico (neg. no. 8191).

VENISON MINCEMEAT PIE

4 cups venison meat, boiled and ground

6 cups diced tart apples

¾ cup raisins

¾ cup currants

½ pint apple jelly

2 cups ground suet

1½ cups stock (preferably the stock in which the
venison was boiled)

1 cup apple cider

2 tablespoons ground cloves

2 tablespoons ground cinnamon

2 tablespoons nutmeg

1 cup sugar

½ teaspoon salt

Brandy to taste

Combine all the ingredients except the brandy and simmer for 1 hour, stirring often. When cool, stir in the brandy.

Store the mincemeat in sterilized jars and keep it cold until ready to use in pies. Makes filling for 2 9-inch pies.

PIE CRUST

2½ cups unsifted flour

1 cup lard or vegetable shortening

1 teaspoon salt

1 teaspoon sugar

1 egg

Blend the first 4 ingredients. Then break the egg into a measuring cup and whip. Add enough cold water to the whipped egg to equal ½ cup. Mix together with the dry ingredients.

To bake mincemeat pie, preheat the oven to 450 degrees. Form the dough into a ball, handling lightly. For a double-crust pie, divide the dough into equal parts. Using a floured wooden board, roll half the dough ⅛ inch thick, working from the center out. Ease the dough into a 9-inch pie pan, pressing down gently. Take care to leave no air between the dough and the pan. Trim off the excess dough with a knife, leaving a 1-inch overhang.

Fill the shell with mincemeat. Roll out anoth-er pie crust and drape it over the filling. Prick the top with a fork. Pinch the edges of the top and bottom dough together. Bake the pie at 450 degrees for 10 minutes; then reduce the heat to 350 degrees and bake another 30 minutes. Makes 1 10-inch double-crust pie.

GINGERBREAD

1½ cups soft shortening

2 tablespoons sugar

1 egg

1 cup molasses

1 cup boiling water

1 teaspoon baking soda

½ teaspoon salt

1 teaspoon ginger

1 teaspoon cinnamon

2¼ cups sifted flour

Preheat the oven to 325 degrees. Mix the short-ening, sugar, and egg. Blend in the molasses and boiling water. Then sift the dry ingredients together and stir into the liquids. Beat until smooth. Pour into a well-greased loaf pan and bake 45 to 50 minutes. Serve hot or cold with whipped cream. Serves 6.

EGGNOG

12 eggs, separated

1½ cups sugar

1 quart cream

1 quart milk

1 quart whiskey

½ cup rum

Nutmeg

Beat the egg yolks separately, adding 1 cup sugar to the yolks as they're beaten; then beat the egg whites, adding ½ cup sugar to them as they're beaten. Fold together the 2 egg mixtures. Next, slowly blend in the cream and milk. Add the whiskey and rum slowly while blending. Serve well chilled with a dash of nutmeg on top. This recipe will fill a large punch bowl.

Christmas in Santa Fe Today

Santa Fe, the epicenter of southwestern style, has long been known for its live and let live philosophy. This relaxed attitude has made it a city of contrasts, where movie stars rub elbows with descendants of the ancient Anasazi and Spanish conquistadors. The city is a haven for free spirits, nonconformists, those wishing to escape the pressures of big cities, and people simply seeking a new way of life.

Americans of all sorts have found their way to Santa Fe since the United States won the territory from Mexico in 1846. Among the first immigrating "Anglos" (a term loosely used to describe almost anyone not of Native American or Hispanic descent) were Lebanese farmers, German-Jewish merchants, Irish cowboys, and a Chinese family that opened both a laundry and a restaurant. This diverse group was joined by mountain men, trappers, and homesteaders of various ethnic backgrounds.

It was the clarity of light that brought artists to the area beginning in the 1920s. Painters such as Georgia O'Keeffe, Marsden Hartley, and John Sloan, as well as photographers Eliot Porter and Laura Gilpin, were all captivated by Santa Fe's compelling charms. Within the last fifty years, Native American and western art have experienced a renaissance—another factor that draws both artists and art lovers to Santa Fe, now the third largest art market in the United States.

In recent years, prominent entertainment figures have arrived from California and New York, along with an influx of wealthy Texans and Oklahomans. In addition, spiritual seekers—Buddhists, Moslems, Catholic monks, and New Age gurus—have all found a home in Santa Fe. It is, after all, the City Different, a melting pot of ideas and cultures.

Santa Fe is a stimulating place to be any time of the year. From spring to early fall, this small cultural mecca bustles with activities. Visitors from all walks of life and every corner of the globe flood the narrow, brick-paved streets surrounding the historic plaza. They come to enjoy the opera, art exhibits, symphony concerts, chamber music, and theater, as well as to attend the annual major events: Indian Market, Spanish Market, the Festival of the Arts, the Rodeo de Santa Fe, the Mountain Man Rendezvous, and the Fiesta de Santa Fe.

By late September, the visitors have thinned out, and the city seems to relax. After the ex-

(Opposite page) The Santa Fe Plaza, laid out in the early 1600s, became known as the "End of the Santa Fe Trail." Transformed by snow and lights during the Christmas season, it provides the setting for pure holiday magic. Photograph © by Scott Christopher.

(Below) Traditional adobe house with turquoise gate. Photograph © by Marcia Keegan.

(Upper left) A leisurely stroll through softly falling snow in the almost deserted plaza. Photograph © by Scott Christopher.

(Center left) Santa Fe, with its adobe architecture, is a unique amalgamation of Native American, Spanish, and Anglo-European traditions. Photograph © by Scott Christopher.

(Right) Indian vendors line the long portal of the Palace of the Governors as they have done for centuries, selling jewelry, pottery, weavings, and other handcrafted items. Photograph © by Joe Maggiore.

(Below) Frontier buildings and territorial- and Pueblo-style shops and galleries offer a wide variety of merchandise to holiday shoppers. Photograph © by Eduardo Fuss.

citement and stimulation of the warm summer and autumn months, the pace becomes slower, more leisurely. The first snowfall and the crisp high-desert air, perfumed by the aroma of piñon burning in fireplaces, spark thoughts of the approaching holiday season.

While it's true that Santa Fe abounds with cultural activities, spectacular scenery, and Old World charm at any time of year, the spell it weaves at Christmas is one of pure enchantment. Dusted with snow, decorated with lights, and wrapped in a warm holiday glow, the City of the Holy Faith celebrates the birth of Christ as it has done for centuries—in its own special way.

Christmas is heralded, as might be expected in the City Different, with an unusual blend of innovative decorations. Whimsical combinations of the traditional and the trendy abound, from spray-painted tumbleweed "snowmen" to holly-clad cow skulls. They meld with time-honored decorations such as *nacimientos* (manger scenes), evergreen branches, red chile *ristras*, and *farolitos* (paper bag lanterns)—resulting in a holiday ambience that is unique to Santa Fe.

Luminarias (bonfires), *farolitos*, *posole* (hominy), and *bizcochitos* (Spanish cookies), are all essential ingredients in a traditional Santa Fe Christmas. Add fresh snow and crisp piñon-scented air; church bells ringing in St. Francis Cathedral; and trees decorated with little white lights, red chiles, and wooden coyotes. Include the centuries-old *Las Posadas* (a Spanish folk drama reenacting Mary and Joseph's search for shelter in Bethlehem) performed in the ancient plaza. Blend in a Christmas Eve stroll along festive Canyon Road and a visit from Santa through your corner *kiva* fireplace. Top it off with Christmas Day ceremonial dances at nearby Indian pueblos, and there you have it—the recipe for *Feliz Navidad* in the City Different. It's an unforgettable experience. Ask anyone who has had the good fortune to be part of the magic of Christmas in Santa Fe.

(Above) The dining room of the historic La Fonda Hotel, decorated for the Christmas holidays. Legend has it that Billy the Kid washed dishes at La Fonda. Today, the hotel provides lodging for visitors from all over the world. Photograph © by Joe Maggiore.

(Left) In Santa Fe, even adults celebrate the season with the joyful spirit of childhood. Photograph © by Eduardo Fuss.

Los Matachines

The masked dance known as *Los Matachines*, performed on Christmas Day in Santa Fe, as well as at many pueblos and nearby Spanish villages, is a colorful blending of European and Native American traditions.

The centuries-old dance was brought to northern New Mexico from Spain through Mexico and has roots in the early history of the Conquest. However, the exotic costumes and dance style probably originated with the Moors who invaded Spain during the eighth century. *Los Matachines* is usually performed to sixteenth-century Spanish folk music played on violins and guitars. Santa Clara Pueblo, however, performs the dance to drums and Native American songs.

Los Matachines *dancers perform in front of St. Francis Cathedral. Photograph © by Jane Mont and Chris Mitchell.*

Pueblo Indian
Christmas Celebrations Today

Pueblo Winter Dances

A variety of dances, most honoring animals such as deer, buffalo, antelope, and mountain sheep, are performed on Christmas Eve or on Christmas Day at the nearby pueblos. These dances are communal prayers meant to ensure the cycle of death and regeneration, as well as to acknowledge the human connection with other species and the environment. Christmas dances are performed in the pueblo plaza, which is the physical, spiritual, and symbolic center of the pueblo world.

Boughs of piñon and other evergreens are often used by Pueblo dancers in their costumes. Symbols of man's relation to all plants, these sprigs of greenery in the winter dances are a reminder that life has not disappeared with winter's darkness but lies dormant awaiting the returning warmth of spring.

Joe S. Sando, in his book *Pueblo Nations: Eight Centuries of Pueblo Indian History*, explains, "In taking branches from the sacred Douglas fir tree, the Pueblo men will inform the Creator that the intent is not to mutilate the tree, but to decorate the human being in the performance of a sacred ritual or dance in His honor. In Pueblo religion, the Douglas fir is used to adorn most dancers, male and female" (page 33).

For the Pueblo Indians, the ancient tradition of winter dances is now interwoven with the comparatively recent celebration of Christmas. As historian Erna Fergusson states in the intro-duction to her book *Dancing Gods*, "This mingling of faiths seems to be due to a quality of mind which makes it possible for the Indian not only to be tolerant of the beliefs of others, but to adopt them into his own practice. [The Indian] seems to feel that every form of worship is good" (page xx).

Visitors should be aware that the Pueblo winter dances are a form of worship not entertainment and behave accordingly. Clapping or loud talking is considered disrespectful. Photographing, videotaping, and sketching are not allowed during many dances. Some pueblos will confiscate cameras if this restriction is ignored. For more information about attending winter dances at the pueblos, see "Christmas Events."

This Pueblo Indian version of Santa Claus demonstrates a unique blend of cultural and religious traditions. Photograph © by Eduardo Fuss.

Other Christmas Celebrations

In addition to ancient dances, Pueblo Indians celebrate the Christmas holidays with traditions borrowed from both the Spanish and Anglo cultures. Midnight Mass and Christmas morning Mass are celebrated. Bonfires are lighted on Christmas Eve to symbolize the coming of the Christ Child.

In a notable example of the melding of two cultures, most pueblos create a plaza shrine for a statue of their Catholic patron saint. Prior to the Christmas dances, a procession sings Spanish hymns while carrying the statue to the altar in the plaza to witness the dances.

Jemez Pueblo celebrates a week-long feast beginning on Christmas Eve, in which a pueblo family acts as "host" to the Christ Child. The host home becomes the center of the village holiday celebration, which includes traditional dances.

Pueblo Christmas trees, a tradition borrowed from the Anglo culture, are often hung with handcrafted pottery decorations.

(Opposite page, top) Deer dancers at San Ildefonso Pueblo. The Deer Dance often starts at night. As dawn breaks, the dancers appear wearing deer antler headdresses and protected from the cold by deer hides. They enter the pueblo from the mountains, dancing to the ancient drum rhythms of their ancestors. Although the dance may appear simple, each variation has its own special and often elaborate steps. Photograph © by Eduardo Fuss.

(Opposite page, bottom) Comanche Dance at Santa Clara Pueblo. Photograph © by Marcia Keegan.

(Left) Deer dancer from San Juan Pueblo. Photograph © by Marcia Keegan.

(Below) Taos Pueblo in winter. Photograph © by Marcia Keegan.

Spanish Christmas Celebrations Today

Christmas is celebrated with a special reverence at the historic village of Chimayó, located twenty-eight miles north of Santa Fe. The legend of the Santuario de Chimayó centers on a crucifix said to have been buried in Chimayó during the 1680 Pueblo Revolt. In 1810, the crucifix was dug up and carried in a joyous procession nine miles to the church at Santa Cruz. Somehow, the story goes, the crucifix was returned to Chimayó. According to legend the cross was taken to Santa Cruz three times, and three times it inexplicably returned to Chimayó. As acknowledgment of the power of this mystery, the Santuario was built on the spot where the crucifix was supposed to have been found.

Through the years, more legends have grown around the famous church. The spot where the crucifix had been buried is said to have soil with great healing powers. The Chimayó soil, samples of which can be taken from a hole in the dirt floor of the tiny sacristy of the church, is collected by people who come from all over the world.

Las Posadas

The tradition of *Las Posadas*, which means the inns or shelters, is an old Spanish miracle play reenacting the biblical story of Joseph and Mary searching for shelter in Bethlehem. Mary is about to give birth. Unfortunately, the

(Opposite page) A December snow dusts the legendary Santuario at the nearby village of Chimayó. Photograph © by Scott Christopher.

(Left) An altar at the Santuario de Chimayó, where the faithful light candles to accompany their Christmas prayers. Photograph © by Scott Christopher.

village inns are full, so after being turned away repeatedly, the couple finds refuge in a manger, where Jesus is born.

Based on the events leading up to the birth of Christ as written by St. Luke, *Las Posadas* originated in medieval Spain and was brought to Mexico four hundred years ago. It is performed throughout New Mexico as well as on the Santa Fe Plaza.

Traditionally, the play continues for nine consecutive evenings before Christmas Eve, from December 16 through December 24. All the dialogue is sung in Spanish. On each evening the couple who portrays Joseph and Mary, followed by a chorus, goes to a designated home to ask for a room. With the exception of the last night, the couple is turned away by the residents (innkeepers) or the devil. However, on the last night the holy couple is granted shelter in a manger.

Contrary to this tradition, the Santa Fe Plaza performance takes place in one evening, usually the Sunday before Christmas. Instead of going to private homes, Joseph and Mary progress around the plaza accompanied by several hundred people—tourists and locals carrying candles. Seeking shelter at various resting places, the couple is mocked by the costumed devil, who in turn evokes hisses and boos from the crowd. The colloquy consists of those singing the lyrics of the "pilgrims" and those singing the part of the "innkeepers." The music and the lyrics are simple so that all may join in, and a musical director coordinates the performance.

The plaza procession ends at the Palace of the Governors, where Mary, Joseph, and the crowd of onlookers are invited inside the courtyard for *bizcochitos,* cider, and the singing of Spanish Christmas carols.

Being a part of *Las Posadas* is a memorable holiday experience for Santa Feans and visitors alike. To many, the ancient performance is a time-honored way of keeping the *fe* (faith) in Santa Fe, the City of the Holy Faith.

Las Posadas*
(An English Translation)

Pilgrims:
From a very long journey,
We've arrived and are weary;
And come to implore you
For shelter this night.

Innkeepers:
Who comes to our door,
On such a cold night?
Who approaches impudently,
And disturbs our rest?

Pilgrims:
Who will give us lodging,
To us, very weary travelers?
We are tired of walking,
And trudging so many roads.

Innkeepers:
Who is it that makes such requests?
I cannot heed such a demand,
For you might just be thieves,
And bent on robbing me!

Pilgrims:
We only intend to rob you
Of the kindness of your heart;
Permit my beloved spouse
A corner in which to rest!

Innkeepers:
Actually there is no room,
In the inn that is empty;
But the countryside is free,
And there's hospitality there!

Pilgrims:
But ours is a grave necessity
To beg at least some shelter,
For my wife needs a room
In which to seek repose!

Innkeepers:
Who is it that disturbs our rest?
And bothers us now in the night?
Go away, go away, please,
And stop robbing us of sleep!

Pilgrims:
But, oh, do take heed,
For the love of God Himself!
My beloved spouse is cold,
And getting more fatigued!

Innkeepers:
Oh, you stubborn people.
You are getting most annoying!
Please depart from this place,
And stop robbing us of sleep!

Pilgrims:
But this beautiful Maiden,
No longer can withstand the cold
She will not be able to withstand,
Weather that becomes more inclement!

Innkeepers:
Certainly you know how late it is!
And coming with such a request
Makes us all the more suspicious!
Go away at once!

Reprinted by permission from Christmas in Old Santa Fe *by Pedro Ribera Ortega, page 13.*

Pilgrims:
The night quickly advances,
In God's name be compassionate!
Do prove some simple rest
For the Queen of Heaven!

Innkeepers:
Your entreaties do annoy us,
And we shall no longer listen;
Seek but an empty field,
And find some shelter there!

Pilgrims:
But 'tis only Joseph and Mary,
His most beloved spouse,
Who, here standing at your door,
Have come seeking lodging!

Innkeepers:
Then enter, most beautiful Maiden!
Thou and thy Spouse, please come in!
For this is thy house, believe me,
And most humbly do we offer it thee!

Pilgrims:
For the hospitality you offer,
For this kindness, God Himself,
Will certainly recompense you and
From heaven will reward you well!

Innkeepers:
Open wide these doors and portals,
Do away with all suspicions,
For here has come to seek repose
The blessed Queen of Heaven!

Pilgrims:
Let happiness and much joy abide,
In this our humble abode, today!
For the travelers are none other
Than a loving spouse named Joseph
With a chaste and lovely Maiden!

Innkeepers:
And since we've been so highly honored,
Assuredly we must perforce give thanks,
Humble thanks we do now give
To Joseph and to Mary.

(Opposite page) A reenactment of Las Posadas. *A young couple playing Mary and Joseph seek shelter at various points around the Santa Fe Plaza. Photograph © by Eduardo Fuss.*

(Left) Las Posadas: *A mischievous "devil" taunts the holy couple and teases onlookers. Photograph © by Eduardo Fuss.*

(Below) Las Posadas *celebration. Photograph © by Eduardo Fuss.*

Our Lady of Guadalupe: The Patroness of the Americas

Deeply rooted in the psyche of New Mexico Catholics is *Nuestra Señora de Guadalupe*, Our Lady of Guadalupe, the official patroness of the entire New World. For many Santa Feans, the Christmas season traditionally begins on December 12 with the centuries-old *Fiesta de la Virgen de Guadalupe*, a celebration that includes vespers, processions, and special Masses at the local Santuario de Guadalupe, the oldest shrine to Our Lady still standing in the United States.

As a symbol for political justice, compassion, and peace, images of Our Lady of Guadalupe can be found throughout the Southwest. They are the subject of religious paintings *(retablos)* and other Spanish folk art, and they decorate stained-glass church windows, as well as candles, T-shirts, business cards, and Christmas ornaments.

According to legend, *La Virgen* first appeared early on the morning of December 9, 1593, outside Mexico City. On a hillside called Tepeyac (once the site of a temple to Tontanzin, the Aztec mother of all gods), Juan Diego, an Indian who had converted to Christianity, encountered a radiant woman who identified herself as the Virgin Mary. She instructed Diego to convince the local bishop to build a church on the site, so that she might tend to her children and remedy their pains and sufferings.

But the skeptical bishop insisted on a sign from heaven. At that point, the Lady instructed Diego to take Castilian roses growing on the frozen hillside to the bishop as proof of her identity. The young Indian followed her instructions, cutting the out-of-season flowers and wrapping them in his *tilma*, or cloak. When he opened his cloak, a vivid image of the Lady appeared on the cloth.

In Mexico, the faithful still flock to view Juan Diego's *tilma*. Woven from a coarse maguey

fiber, the sacred garment is still intact after almost five hundred years. It is enshrined at the basilica built in the Virgin's honor.

The story of the Virgin of Guadalupe was brought to New Mexico with the conquistadors. Her ideals, which reflect a peaceful blending of cultures, have also been revered by generations of Pueblo Indians. The pueblos of Pojoaque and Jemez traditionally celebrate an annual Feast of Guadalupe. Schedules for the dances vary from year to year; check with the

La Conquistadora: Our Lady of the Conquest

Known as *La Conquistadora*, queen and patroness of the ancient kingdom of New Mexico and its villa of Santa Fe, this centuries-old statue is America's oldest Madonna and an integral part of Santa Fe history.

No one knows for sure when she was originally brought to New Mexico; however, according to legend, she was carved in Mexico and brought to New Mexico in 1625 by Fray Alonso de Benavides and the conquistadors. Originally known as Our Lady of the Assumption, she was renamed *La Conquistadora*, Our Lady of the Conquest, after she was taken from Santa Fe by survivors of the Pueblo Revolt in 1680 and returned by Don Diego de Vargas when he reconquered the city in 1692.

The sacred statue resides in the north chapel of St. Francis Cathedral. At Christmas time, she is dressed in gold robes and a magnificent crown and holds an ancient *Niño Jesús*, statue of

(Opposite page) Our Lady of Guadalupe. Detail of a large mural on Guadalupe Street in Santa Fe titled Gift to the People of Santa Fe. *It was designed by Jeremy Morrelli and painted by Alexander Rokoff. Materials were supplied by Wellborn Paint Store. Photograph © by Marcia Keegan.*

(Right) Statue of La Conquistadora. *Photograph © by Eduardo Fuss.*

The Famed Miraculous Staircase at Loretto Chapel

Visitors flock year-round to the small Loretto Chapel just south of the plaza, on Old Santa Fe Trail. They come to admire the elegant French Gothic-style architecture. But most of all, they come to view the chapel's famed "miraculous" staircase.

Whether or not the construction actually involved a miracle, the steep, coiled wooden staircase with its two complete 360-degree turns is a masterpiece of carpentry. Many believe that's because the carpenter was none other than St. Joseph, the patron saint of carpenters.

The Chapel of Our Lady of the Light, better known as Loretto Chapel, was built in 1873 for the Sisters of Loretto, who had traveled from Kentucky to Santa Fe to establish a convent under the direction of Archbishop Jean Baptiste Lamy. The nuns also established the Loretto Academy for Girls (now the site of the Inn at Loretto) that operated until 1968.

Construction of the chapel by French and Italian stonemasons, who later built the St. Francis Cathedral, took five years. When completed, the chapel had a choir loft but no stairway to get to it. The Sisters of Loretto prayed to St. Joseph for help. According to legend, their prayers were promptly answered by a man who arrived with a donkey and only three tools—a saw, a T square, and a hammer. After constructing the staircase, which has neither a center support nor nails, the mysterious carpenter refused payment for his labor and disappeared.

Among the special delights of Christmas in Santa Fe are Christmas concerts performed in the chapel by such groups as the Santa Fe Pro Musica (the combined organization of the Orchestra of Santa Fe and Ensemble of Santa Fe), the Santa Fe Desert Chorale, and the Santa Fe Women's Ensemble. The chapel is open 9 A.M. to 5 P.M. every day except Christmas.

(Above) The miraculous staircase at Loretto Chapel. Photograph © by Eduardo Fuss.

(Opposite) St. Francis Cathedral was built at the direction of Archbishop Jean Baptiste Lamy, who arrived in Santa Fe from France in 1851. The celebration of Christmas Eve Midnight Mass at St. Francis Cathedral is a cherished Santa Fe tradition for people of all faiths. Photograph © by Scott Christopher.

A Santa Fe Christmas with Richard Clawson

As a world traveler, Richard has celebrated Christmas all over the globe. "I was always searching for the perfect Christmas," he said. "I've spent the holiday in many exciting places—New York, London, Berlin, Paris, Zurich, and Spain. After spending my first Christmas in the ancient city of Santa Fe, I knew that my search had ended. I had finally found the most traditional and unique celebration of all. My wish is to share this joyful experience with people everywhere through this book."

For Richard, Christmas is associated with many memories of his grandmother, Anna Rose Laughridge. She was a descendant of the oldest Irish family in America, and had a strong sense of tradition and a special fondness of the Christmas season.

The daughter of a country doctor, she came from Kansas to California during the Great Depression with her husband and six children. Among her most treasured possessions was her collection of Christmas ornaments. Although she was forced to sell most of her belongings before the move, she refused to part with her Christmas ornaments and tied them on the top of the family Model T.

"Mom," as she was called, "always had a large Christmas tree," Richard remembers. "It was decorated ceiling to floor with her wonderful ornaments. The holidays were such a special time to her."

Among Richard's favorite childhood memories is the smell of Mom's Christmas baking.

"The wonderful, sweet, yeasty smell would permeate the entire house," he said. "After dinner, we would gather around the fireplace while she sang Irish lullabies and told magical stories. My favorite story was one about seeing ladies dancing in the firelight."

Preparing for Christmas

Every year Richard looks forward to Christmas with anticipation. "The magic of the holiday season fills me with great excitement," he said, as he decorated the portal of his home with fresh greens and bright red chiles.

"Just after Thanksgiving, I go into high gear," he continued. One of the first things he does is to unwrap his grandmother's old Christmas ornaments. "A love of the holiday season was my grandmother's greatest gift to me," he said. "And,

(Opposite page) Richard places several Christmas trees throughout his home, each with its own southwestern theme. Here he incorporates cranberry-chile garlands and Mexican tin and papier mâché ornaments with cowboy and Indian artifacts. His cavalier King Charles spaniels, Katie and Finnegan, enjoy the holiday excitement from a comfortable chair. Photograph © by Joe Maggiore.

(Left) Christmas is for the child in all of us. Christmas Eve, 1948; Richard's grandmother, "Mom," reading to Richard and his cousin, Sharyn Carr. Photograph courtesy of Richard Clawson.

through the years, I've carried her Irish traditions, recipes, and decorations to the many different countries in the world where I've spent Christmas. But never have my family traditions meant as much to me as they do here in Santa Fe, where Christmas reflects the happy blending of many diverse cultures." But he adds: "The warmth and magic of a Santa Fe Christmas is in the heart and can be re-created wherever you live."

Fill the House with Christmas

To celebrate the holidays, Richard fills his entry hall with edible treats. For example, he puts chunks of Grandma's Piñon Nut Brittle (see page 111 for recipe) in clear cellophane bags tied with raffia bows. Included is the note: "From *mi casa* to *su casa*: Candy made with piñon nuts from the City Different just for you." The

A time-worn hutch is crowned with Indian pottery, Hopi kachinas, naturally shed deer antlers, chile, cranberry garlands, fresh eucalyptus, and pine boughs. Photograph © by Joe Maggiore.

candy is then placed in a large Indian basket. Departing guests are urged to help themselves.

Homes should smell as good as they look during the holidays. Richard advises using lots of scented candles. "Candles lighten the mood of a room," he said. "They'll make your Christmas memories burn that much brighter!"

He also fills his kitchen with yuletide aromas by simmering citrus peel, nutmeg, cloves, and cinnamon sticks in a saucepan on the stove. (Use the recipe for Mulled Wine, page 110, and substitute water for wine.) In addition, he keeps a stack of scented pinecones near the fireplace, ready to be tossed into the fire. This is a great way to permeate a room with the special fragrance of Christmas.

below 70 degrees and nighttime temperatures are from 60 to 65 degrees. Set the plants in bright, indirect light, and keep the soil around them moderately moist. Both leaves and flowers are moderately poisonous, so keep them out of reach of small children and pets. Richard clusters poinsettias in groups of three or more for the most dramatic impact at Christmas time.

In the following pages, you are invited into Richard's home to experience the magic of a Santa Fe-style Christmas as he combines personal traditions, treasures, and recipes with those of the American Southwest. He designs parties—with recipes, decorations, and table settings—for a variety of holiday gatherings. He also provides instructions for making innovative southwestern food and crafts for gift giving.

Deck the House with Holiday Flowers

Richard begins holiday preparations weeks before Christmas by "forcing" bulbs to grow and bloom early. Amaryllis and paper-white narcissus add color and scent to festive arrangements and respond nicely to being forced.

Check with your local nursery for bulbs suitable for forcing. Amaryllis will take nine to ten weeks to bloom. Plant the bulbs in an all-purpose potting mixture, with one part sand. One-third of the bulb should be above the soil. Plant the bulbs in clusters of three or more. Keep them moist.

Paper-white narcissus will need about four weeks to blossom. Set the bulbs on a bed of gravel and add enough water to touch the bottom of the bulbs.

For most households, holiday decorating means displaying a few poinsettias, known locally as *flor de Noche Buena*, the flower of Christmas Eve. Among the most beautiful are Freedom poinsettias, a rich-looking, hardy variety which should last well into spring. These plants do best when daytime temperatures indoors stay

(Top) An antique Mexican serape, a colorful Mexican folk art lizard by artist Antonio Mandarin, nineteenth-century Spanish candleholders, raffia-tied candles, and a plate of Silvered Fruit (see page 107 for directions) decorate Richard's living room coffee table at Christmas. Photograph © by Joe Maggiore.

(Bottom) The focal point of this Christmas arrangement is a large antique santo of St. Joseph on a burro, surrounded by bright red amaryllis, candles, and a ceramic nacimiento *from Mexico. Photograph © by Joe Maggiore.*

Holiday Open House Buffet

As the oldest capital city in the United States, Santa Fe is steeped in history. As a major art center, it has more galleries and artists per capita than any city in the world.

Holiday gallery parties are popular events that range from the simple to the elegant. They are great opportunities to meet with friends, enjoy good food, and see what's new on the Santa Fe art scene at the same time. On the following pages, Richard designs an Open House Buffet at Nedra Matteucci's Fenn Galleries.

Menu

Mulled Cider
Spicy Red Salsa with
Southwest Tortilla Chips
Black Bean Dip
Guacamole
Build-Your-Own Tostados
Pork and Pumpkin Empanadas
Chile Rice Navidad
Bread Pudding
Mexican Coffee

Recipes

MULLED CIDER

Follow the recipe for Mulled Wine (page 110), substituting cider for wine.

SPICY RED SALSA

4 large tomatoes (about 2 pounds), chopped

3 large green bell peppers, seeded and chopped

1 medium yellow onion, chopped

1–2 jalapeño chiles, seeded and minced

¼ cup cilantro, chopped

1 teaspoon ground cumin

2 tablespoons fresh lime juice

3 cloves garlic, minced

Salt to taste

Combine all the ingredients and mix; the mixture should be chunky. Let it stand 15 minutes and serve with Southwest Tortilla Chips. Makes 1½ cups.

SOUTHWEST TORTILLA CHIPS

Assorted Southwest-style cookie cutters

2 dozen fresh yellow corn tortillas

2 dozen fresh blue corn tortillas

1 cup vegetable oil

Salt to taste

Press the cookie cutters into the soft tortillas to make the desired shapes. Preheat the oil and fry the corn chips until crisp (about 3 minutes), turning often. Drain on paper towels. Salt and serve with dips and/or salsa. Serves 24.

BLACK BEAN DIP
(Use also as ingredient in
Build-Your-Own Tostados)

2 tablespoons olive oil

¾ cup yellow onion, chopped

4 cups cooked (or canned) well-drained black beans

(Opposite page) The focal point of this imaginative table setting is an antique English Victorian rocking horse sitting on a bed of fresh pine boughs, red chiles, and an Indian saddle blanket. Adding to the festive southwestern mood are vibrant lilies and Mexican tin candleholders. The tree in the background is festooned with small white lights, raffia garlands, and Richard's heirloom Christmas ornaments. Photograph © by Jane Mont and Chris Mitchell.

(Above) Close-up of Black Bean Dip decorated with fresh chiles. Photograph © by Jane Mont and Chris Mitchell.

1 large bell pepper, chopped

1 jalapeño chile, seeded and chopped

1 large tomato, chopped

3 tablespoons fresh cilantro, chopped

2 tablespoons balsamic vinegar

2 tablespoons lime juice

Heat the oil in a medium skillet. Sauté the onion about 4 minutes. Add the cooked beans, bell pepper, and *jalapeño* chile and cook for another 5 minutes. Partially mash the beans. Combine the tomato, cilantro, vinegar, and lime juice and mix well. Decorate with a fresh chile and cilantro sprigs. Serve at room temperature with Southwest Tortilla Chips (page 55). Makes 5 cups.

GUACAMOLE

6 ripe avocados

Juice from 2 fresh limes

2 large yellow onions, finely chopped

6 cloves garlic, minced

4 jalapeño chiles, seeded and finely chopped

2 large tomatoes, chopped

1/2 cup fresh cilantro, chopped

6–8 drops Tabasco sauce

Salt and pepper to taste

Lime wedges and a red chile for garnish

Peel and pit the avocados. Mash them coarsely with a fork. Combine the lime juice, onions, garlic, chiles, tomatoes, cilantro, Tabasco sauce, salt, and pepper. Garnish with lime wedges and a whole red chile. Serve with Southwest Tortilla Chips (page 55). Makes 3 cups.

BUILD-YOUR-OWN TOSTADOS

1 cup vegetable oil

1 dozen flour tortillas

4 cups Guacamole (above)

4 cups Black Bean Dip (page 55)

3 cups Monterey Jack cheese, shredded

2 roasted red bell peppers, chopped (page 57)

1 1/2 cups sour cream

1 1/2 cups Spicy Red Salsa (page 55)

1 1/2 cups Tomatillo Salsa (page 63)

2 heads romaine lettuce, shredded

Heat the oil in a skillet and fry the tortillas about 3 minutes until golden brown. Drain on paper towels. To serve, fill separate bowls with Guacamole, Black Bean Dip, cheese, bell peppers, sour cream, salsas, and lettuce. Arrange tortillas in a basket in an upright position. Let your guests build their own treat. Makes 12 *tostados*.

PORK AND PUMPKIN EMPANADAS

Dough

1 2/3 cups all-purpose flour

1/8 teaspoon salt

4 ounces butter or margarine

1/3 cup milk

Sift the dry ingredients into a bowl and cut in the butter or margarine using your fingers or 2 forks. Add the milk and mix just enough so the dough can be formed easily into a ball. Refrigerate for at least 1 hour.

Filling

3 tablespoons olive oil

2 large yellow onions, finely chopped

3 cloves fresh garlic, minced

2 roasted red bell peppers, seeded, stemmed, and finely chopped (see page 57)

1 jalapeño chile, seeded and minced

2 pounds ground pork

2 medium potatoes, peeled, boiled, and chopped

4 tablespoons fresh parsley

Guests choose their own toppings to make Build-Your-Own Tostados. Photograph © by Jane Mont and Chris Mitchell.

6 tablespoons (½ cup) canned pumpkin

¼ teaspoon red pepper flakes

1 teaspoon ground nutmeg

⅓ cup brown sugar

Glaze

1 egg, beaten

1 tablespoon milk

Using a medium skillet, sauté the onions and garlic for 3 to 4 minutes in ½ of the oil. Add the red bell peppers and *jalapeño* chile. Cook until the onions are golden brown.

In another skillet, sauté the pork in the remaining oil until well done, stirring frequently. Stir into the onion mixture. Combine all the other filling ingredients and mix well.

Preheat the oven to 400 degrees. Divide the dough into 2 parts and roll out to a thickness of ⅛ inch. Cut into 6-inch circles. Spoon the filling onto ½ the circle. Brush the edges with the beaten egg and fold the other half of the circle over the filling so that the edges meet. Press a fork into the edges to seal the *empanadas.*

Bake for 10 minutes on an ungreased baking sheet. Reduce the heat to 350 degrees and bake until light brown. Brush with egg and milk glaze and bake an additional 5 minutes. Serves 10.

ROASTING CHILES AND PEPPERS

To roast chiles or peppers, arrange them on a broiler pan or grill rack and roast 2 to 3 inches from the heat, turning until blistered. In a paper bag, let them steam and cool, then peel, core, and seed. Wear rubber gloves when handling chiles since they can burn the skin.

CHILE RICE NAVIDAD

½ cup chopped onions

½ stick butter

1½ cups uncooked, washed white rice
   (California pearl works best)

3–4 cups hot chicken stock or broth (page 95)

Pinch of saffron

Sauté the onions in the butter. Add the rice and stir well. Pour in the hot chicken stock and saffron

and bring the mixture to a boil. Cover and simmer for 15 minutes. While the rice is cooking, assemble the following ingredients:

1 pint sour cream

1 roasted red bell pepper, chopped (see above)

1 6-ounce can green chiles

3–4 drops Tabasco sauce

1 cup Monterey Jack or sharp cheddar cheese, diced

¼ cup fresh green onions, chopped

Mix the sour cream with the chopped bell pepper, green chiles, Tabasco sauce, and diced cheese. Remove the rice from the stove and pour in ½ the sour cream mixture. Pour into a buttered 8 x 10-inch baking dish. Top with the remaining sour cream mixture. Bake in a 350-degree oven for about 15 minutes, until golden brown. Sprinkle with chopped green onions. Serves 6 to 8.

A bowl of Chile Rice Navidad sits on an antique matador's cape. The museum-quality cape is from southern Spain and hand-embroidered with real silver. Photograph © by Joe Maggiore.

BREAD PUDDING

3 whole eggs

1 cup packed brown sugar

¾ cup granulated sugar

¼ cup melted butter

1 cup heavy cream

1 cup eggnog

1 cup milk

¼ cup dark Myers's rum

1 tablespoon vanilla

½ cup yellow raisins

2–3 pears, diced

1 day-old French baguette, cut into ½-inch cubes

Baby pears and kumquats for garnish

Combine the eggs, ½ cup brown sugar, the granulated sugar, the butter, cream, eggnog, milk, rum, and vanilla. Add the raisins and pears. Gently fold in the bread cubes until the mixture is absorbed. Let rest 10 to 15 minutes.

Preheat the oven to 350 degrees. Spread the mixture in a prebuttered 4 x 5-inch loaf pan. Sprinkle the remaining ½ cup brown sugar on top and cover with foil. Place in a larger baking pan and fill it ⅔ up the side with boiling water. Bake for about 1 hour.

Serve warm with whipped cream, garnished with baby pears and kumquats. Also delicious with warm maple syrup and vanilla ice cream. Serves 8.

MEXICAN COFFEE

1 package dark chocolate (approximately 6 ounces)

Coffee, drip-grind for 12-cup coffeemaker

12 4-inch whole cinnamon sticks

⅛ teaspoon ground cloves

1 tablespoon shredded orange peel

4 tablespoons packed brown sugar

Melt the chocolate in a double boiler. Dip the cinnamon sticks into the chocolate, coating ¾ of the way up.

Place the coffee in a filter with the cloves and orange peel and brew according to the manufacturer's directions. Stir in the sugar and serve with a chocolate-covered cinnamon stick for each cup. Swirl and enjoy! Serves 10 to 12.

(Opposite page) Red tulips and banks of poinsettias form the background for this time-tested recipe for Bread Pudding. Photograph © by Joe Maggiore.

(Above) The Basket Dance by Glenna Goodacre. Courtesy of Nedra Matteucci's Fenn Galleries. Photograph © by Marcia Keegan.

Trim a Tree Party

As an ancient symbol of life, the evergreen tree belongs to a tradition far older than Christianity. The practice of decorating trees goes back thousands of years and is associated with many cultures. The ancient Egyptians brought green palm fronds into their homes on the shortest day of the year in December as a symbol of life's triumph over death. Both the Druids and the Romans decorated trees in honor of their gods. But it was in medieval Germany that the custom acquired a Christian context.

The tradition of the decorated Christmas tree spread through Europe and was brought to the United States by Hessian mercenaries paid to fight in the Revolutionary War and later by German settlers.

The popularity of the Christmas tree grew. As settlers came west along the famed Santa Fe Trail, they brought their Christmas traditions with them. With the arrival of the Atchison, Topeka and Santa Fe Railway in 1880, the decorated Christmas tree was soon an accepted part of the City Different's multicultural celebration.

Nothing gets us in a Christmas mood like trimming a tree so why not make a party of it? Good friends and delicious food are a never-fail combination for a special holiday gathering.

In this chapter, Richard demonstrates how to make your tree trimming a social highlight of the yuletide season.

Richard enjoys creating new traditions and incorporating old ones into his holiday celebrations, such as his Trim a Tree Party. A favorite adaptation of an old German custom is that of decorating an outdoor tree for the birds. At this time of year when food for birds is scarce, he always starts his Trim a Tree Party by thinking first of the birds.

Early arrivals to the party are given miniature lights and bird nests with which to decorate the outdoor tree. When all of the guests have arrived, everyone is given a paper cone filled with birdseed. Just before sunset, the party moves to the outdoor tree, where guests fill the bird nests with birdseed.

"With a little bit of luck," Richard says, "we can watch the first birds arriving to eat the birdseed through the living room window. Everyone enjoys that!"

To decorate the indoor tree, Richard passes out large baskets of cherished ornaments with hooks in place and ready to hang. At the end of the Trim a Tree Party, departing guests are given

(Opposite page) Photograph © by Paul De Domenico.

(Left) Santa Feans Arny and Judy Katz, and Susan La Point prepare to trim an outdoor tree for the birds by filling nests with birdseed. Photograph © by Joe Maggiore.

a nest to take home for their own tree, along with the following note: "According to an old German legend, if you find a bird nest in the tree that you harvest for Christmas, you will have an entire year of health and happiness. Tuck this nest in the branches of your tree with all the best wishes of the old legend."

The idea of decorating a tree for the birds at Christmas time also puts us in touch with an important aspect of Santa Fe's Spanish heritage—St. Francis of Assisi, the patron saint of animals as well as of the city of Santa Fe. St. Francis holds a special place in the hearts of Santa Feans during the holiday season.

Menu

Mulled Wine (page 110)
Santa Fe Sunset Dip
Tomatillo Salsa and Spicy Red Salsa (page 55)
Served with Southwest
Tortilla Chips (page 55)
Cocas (Little Spanish Pizzas)
Christmas Coleslaw with
Pepper Dressing
Bizcochitos (page 73)
Coffee Granite
Spanish Coffee

Recipes

SANTA FE SUNSET DIP

1 head garlic, roasted (see page 96)
3 roasted red bell peppers, chopped (see page 57)
2 teaspoons extra virgin olive oil
½ teaspoon ground cumin
6 ounces cream cheese, softened
3 tablespoons cottage cheese
Salt and pepper to taste
Assorted vegetables, cut into dipping size
Fresh kale leaves
Red pepper for garnish

Mix all but the last 3 ingredients with a fork until blended or pulse in a food processor for 30 seconds. Cluster the fresh kale leaves around a stemmed bowl and tie with raffia to form an open flower. Heap the dip inside the bowl and garnish with a red pepper. Sit the stemmed bowl in the center of a platter and arrange the fresh vegetables around the dip. This beautiful dish may also double as a centerpiece. Makes about 1½ cups.

TOMATILLO SALSA

1 pound tomatillos, husked and chopped
3 serrano chiles, seeded and chopped (use more for a
*   spicier sauce)*
2 cloves garlic, chopped
1 medium onion, chopped
1 cup chopped cilantro
1 cup chopped Italian parsley
Juice of 1 lemon
Salt to taste

Put all the ingredients in a large bowl and mix thoroughly. Pour into a blender or food processor and blend at high speed until the salsa is a coarse purée. Refrigerate in a covered container for up to 4 hours before serving. Serve with Southwest Tortilla Chips (page 55). Makes 2 to 3 cups.

(Opposite page) After the tree is decorated, guests enjoy a Santa Fe-style buffet. A southwestern Santa by artist Shelee Robertson, old Navajo rug, and colorful Mexican serape set the holiday mood. Photograph © by Joe Maggiore.

(Above) As they trim the tree, guests help themselves to Mulled Wine and Richard's tasty appetizers. Photograph © by Joe Maggiore.

Little Spanish-style pizzas called Cocas, *individually created and served on glazed Mexican pottery, are a big hit with Trim a Tree Party guests. Close-up of* Coca *slice. Photograph © by Joe Maggiore.*

COCAS (Little Spanish Pizzas)

Dough

3 teaspoons active dry yeast

12 tablespoons warm water (110 degrees)

2 tablespoons fine cornmeal

12 tablespoons whole milk

4 tablespoons extra virgin olive oil

1 teaspoon salt

2 tablespoons rye flour

3½ cups unbleached white flour

Fillings

1 cup roasted red bell peppers (page 57), chopped

1 cup New Mexico or Anaheim chiles, chopped

1 cup red onion, chopped

1 cup black olives, chopped

1 cup corn, grilled and removed from cob,
    or substitute frozen corn nibblets

1 cup cooked (preferably grilled) and
    shredded chicken breast

¼ cup goat cheese

½ cup Monterey Jack cheese, shredded

½ cup chopped cilantro

Dry red pepper flakes in shaker

¼ cup olive oil to brush over pizza dough when
    shaped, and on edges after it comes out
    of the oven

Place the yeast in a small bowl. Dissolve it in the warm water and set it in a warm place for 4 minutes. Combine the cornmeal, milk, and oil in a large mixing bowl. Add the yeast mixture, salt, and rye flour and mix well. Then gradually add the white flour until the dough is soft and workable.

Turn out onto a lightly floured surface and knead for 5 minutes. Sprinkle with a little flour as needed to keep the dough from sticking to the surface. Place the dough in a heavy oiled bowl and turn the dough once so it is coated with oil. Let the dough rise in a warm place until it has doubled in size, about 40 to 45 minutes.

Preheat the oven to 500 degrees at least 30 minutes with a pizza stone on the lower third of the oven. To form the *Cocas*, divide the dough into 4 equal balls. Roll out on a lightly floured surface, turning to keep the shape round. Roll the dough to about ⅛ inch thickness, slightly thicker at the edges.

Lay the dough on an oiled pizza pan or cornmeal-dusted wooden peel. Brush with olive oil. Use any desired combination of fillings listed above. Sprinkle cheese over the *Cocas*, place them in the oven on the pizza stone, and bake for 10 minutes or until golden brown. Brush the edges with oil and sprinkle with chopped cilantro and/or dry red pepper flakes. Serves 4 to 6.

Note: A very hot oven is needed to cook pizzas and *Cocas*. To ensure the proper temperature, use a pizza stone (available at cook stores).

CHRISTMAS COLESLAW WITH PEPPER DRESSING

2 cups green cabbage, shredded

2 cups red cabbage, shredded

¾ cup carrots, shredded

1 each red, yellow, and green bell pepper,
  cored, seeded, and diced

½ cup red onion, chopped

½ cup green onion, chopped

PEPPER DRESSING

1 red chile, seeded, stemmed, and minced,
  or substitute ½ teaspoon red chile flakes

1 cup mayonnaise

1 tablespoon lime juice

2 tablespoons cider vinegar

3 tablespoons honey (fireweed honey is best)

Salt and pepper to taste

Combine the cabbage, carrots, peppers, and onion in a large bowl. Add the dressing ingredients and mix thoroughly. Sprinkle a few green onions on top. Serves 6 to 8.

COFFEE GRANITE

4 cups espresso or strong coffee

¼ cup sugar, or to taste

2 tablespoons Kahlua

1 quart rich vanilla ice cream

¼ pound chocolate-covered espresso beans

Add the sugar to the hot coffee until dissolved. Add the Kahlua and stir. Transfer to a 9 x 13 x 2-inch glass baking dish. Place in the freezer. When partially frozen, stir with the tines of a fork. Spread the mixture out evenly and repeat every 2 hours 3 or 4 times. Stir again just before serving. Spoon into stemmed glasses and top with a scoop of vanilla ice cream. Drizzle a little Kahlua on top and press in 3 chocolate-covered espresso beans. Serve immediately with *Bizcochitos* (page 73). Serves 4 to 6.

SPANISH COFFEE

Use your favorite strong coffee, mixed with Spanish brandy (optional). Stir with cinnamon sticks dipped in dark semisweet chocolate (see page 59 for directions).

Your Christmas Tree

HINTS FOR BUYING THE BEST TREE

Natural trees are a renewable, recyclable resource. Artificial trees often contain non-biodegradable plastics and metals. For every Christmas tree harvested, two to three seedlings are planted in its place. There are about one million acres of Christmas trees being produced in the United States.

Before purchasing a tree, do a freshness test. A tree's needles should be resilient. Hold a branch about six inches from the tip. Pull your hand toward the tip, allowing the branch to slip through your fingers. The needles should adhere to the branch and not fall off in your hand. A good fragrance and healthy green color are other indications of freshness.

Coffee Granite, Bizcochitos, *and Spanish Coffee complete the Trim a Tree Party buffet. Photograph © by Joe Maggiore.*

KEEPING THE TREE FRESH

Remember that natural trees need water the same as a fresh bouquet of flowers does. Make a fresh cut across the base of the trunk about one-fourth inch deep. When a tree is cut, a seal of sap occurs naturally over its stump, which keeps moisture in the tree. It's important to break that seal to allow the tree to "drink" in the water needed to keep it fresh during the holidays.

Place the tree in a water-holding stand immediately. Keep plenty of water in your stand. A Christmas tree may absorb a gallon of water in the first twenty-four hours that it's up and several quarts of water thereafter.

Position your tree away from heat sources such as fireplaces and radiators. Be sure all light cords and connections for tree lights are in good working condition and not frayed. Test each string of lights by plugging it in and replace any burned-out bulbs before you decorate the tree. All bulbs should face outward so they do not come in contact with the needles. Also, paper and other flammable ornaments should never touch Christmas tree lights. Finally, always unplug the lights when you go to bed or leave the house.

Christmas trees are biodegradable. The branches can be removed and used as mulch in the garden. The trunk can be used for firewood or chopped up for mulch.

Today, many people are opting to purchase a live Christmas tree. If you choose to do this, remember that a live tree is more likely to survive if it is a variety that grows naturally in your region. The tree will need several days to acclimate to indoor conditions. This is best accomplished by gradually moving it to warmer locations.

In the house, set the tree container or burlapped root ball in a large pan with sides. When the surface of the burlap or soil is dry to the touch, water the tree to soak the entire root ball. Also, with a live tree you must take care to use the proper lights so as not to damage the branches. Miniature blinking lights generate the least amount of heat and are least likely to singe the needles.

Three weeks is the maximum recommended time that live trees should be kept indoors. After this you should reacclimate the tree to outdoor conditions by placing it on a shaded porch or patio for at least a week. Whether you plan to plant the tree or leave it in its container to be part of next year's Christmas celebration, check with your local nursery for further instructions.

GUIDELINES
FOR A SIMPLY DECORATED TREE

For very small trees, 2- to 4-foot, you will need 50 to 100 lights, 3 to 4 ropes of swag, and 24 to 36 ornaments.

For a 4- to 6-foot tree, you will need 150 to 200 lights, 4 to 5 ropes of swag, and 36 to 48 ornaments.

For a 6- to-8-foot tree, you will need 200 to 400 lights, 5 to 6 ropes of swag, and 48 to 72 ornaments.

(Opposite page) Garden statue of St. Francis. Photograph © by Christopher Watt.

(Left) Snow-covered trees in the Sangre de Cristo Mountains. Photograph © by Scott Christopher.

Prayer to St. Francis at Christmas Time*

Francis of Assisi, gentle Saint—
Who loved your brother men,
Who loved all brother creatures—
Francis, Little Brother,
Who loved the Feast of Christmas
And fashioned, long ago, a Christmas manger,
That your brother men and birds and beasts
Might see and live the beautiful story
Of the birth of the little Lord Jesus—
Might join in worship and praise—
Little Brother of us all,
Come, walk the earth once more!
Come, with your eagerness and joy,
To show earth's children how to live
And laugh and sing, in love, together—
Gentle Francis of Assisi,
Come, teach us how to fashion
And keep within each heart
A Christmas Manger!

— Dorothy A. Linney

*Reprinted courtesy *New Mexico* Magazine

Children's Party

Among Richard's favorite holiday parties is one he plans just for his grandchildren each year. Such parties appeal to the child in all of us. "It's a special family occasion," he said, "an afternoon spent baking cookies, drinking hot chocolate, breaking a Christmas *piñata*, and telling stories around the fire."

In this chapter Richard shares his ideas and recipes for creating a cherished family tradition that will be passed on from generation to generation.

What's a favorite family Christmas tradition? Any member of any family will probably respond, "Making cookies!" That's because children of all ages and cultures agree—nothing tastes better than a homemade cookie warm from the oven.

Menu

Christmas Coyote Cookies
Holiday Hot Chocolate

Recipes

CHRISTMAS COYOTE COOKIES

⅓ cup butter
⅓ cup shortening
¾ cup sugar
1 teaspoon baking powder
Dash of salt

1 egg
1 teaspoon vanilla
1 tablespoon milk
2 cups all-purpose flour
Food coloring in assorted colors
Several coyote-shaped cookie cutters (choose ones with thick necks so that the cookies' heads don't snap off easily). Refer to the coyote pattern (page 127).

Using an electric mixer on medium speed, beat the butter and shortening together for about 30 seconds. Add the sugar, baking powder, salt, egg, vanilla, and milk, beating until well mixed.

Beat in the flour. Set aside ¼ of the dough to color with food coloring. Divide this dough evenly into 4 balls. Add a few drops of food coloring, 1 color for each ball. Blend in with a fork. Wrap the colored dough balls and plain dough in plastic wrap and refrigerate until it is easy to handle.

When chilled, gently press pieces of colored dough randomly into the plain dough mixture. (If the dough is handled too much, return it to the refrigerator and chill it again. The dough must be chilled to work with it.)

Roll out the dough to ⅛-inch thickness. Cut the dough with the coyote cookie cutters, dipping the cutters into flour before each cut. Using a large spatula, place the coyote cookies on a cookie sheet about 2 inches apart.

Bake in a 375-degree oven for 7 to 8 minutes or until the edges are firm and the bottoms are lightly browned. Remove and cool on a sheet of waxed paper. Tie a raffia bow around each coyote's

(Opposite page) Making Christmas Coyote Cookies is almost as much fun as eating them! Shown here are Richard Clawson with his grandchildren Jessica, Christopher, and Amanda Church. Photograph © by Joe Maggiore.

neck and serve. Makes 12 to 18 cookies, depending on the size of the cookie cutters.

Note: To save time, buy ready-made sugar cookie dough and add food coloring.

HOLIDAY HOT CHOCOLATE

½ cup sugar

¼ cup cocoa powder

1½ cups cold water

1 teaspoon ground cinnamon

¾ teaspoon ground cloves

6 cups milk

2 tablespoons vanilla

Whipped cream

Combine the sugar, cocoa, water, cinnamon, and cloves. Mix and simmer for 5 minutes. Slowly add the milk and heat until just scalded. Do not boil. Stir continually until smooth. Mix in the vanilla. Place in warm mugs and top with whipped cream. This recipe is a cold weather favorite with children of all ages. Serves 6.

Piñatas: A Highlight of Children's Holiday Parties

Piñatas, an ancient tradition imported from Mexico by way of Spain, are traditionally a part of children's holiday parties in the City Different. The star of Bethlehem (a round shape decorated with cones to resemble a star) is an especially popular Christmas *piñata*.

A popular example of Hispanic folk art, brightly colored papier-mâché *piñatas* have hollow cores and are filled with candy and other goodies. A *piñata* is suspended from the ceiling by a rope. Blindfolded children swing at it, using a decorated stick. Once the *piñata* is broken open, the children dash forward to grab the treats.

Jessica Church, one of Richard Clawson's grandchildren. Photograph © by Joe Maggiore.

HOW TO MAKE YOUR OWN PIÑATA

Although *piñatas* are traditionally constructed by covering a clay pot with colored tissue paper, a modern method is to make them out of papier-mâché. Using this method, children can have fun constructing their own holiday *piñata* prior to the party.

Materials:

Large balloon and string

Flour

Water

Newspaper

Colored tissue paper, cut into 2-inch strips

Wrapped candy and other small treats

Masking tape

Instructions: Blow up the balloon and tie it with a 3-foot string. Mix the flour and water to form a thick, lumpy paste. Cover the balloon with strips of newspaper that have been dipped into the papier-mâché paste. Cover the balloon with several layers, finishing with a layer of tissue paper of desired colors. To make a star of Bethlehem *piñata*, glue on cones made of construction paper and cover them with paper strips. Hang the *piñata* from the string to dry.

After the *piñata* is completely dry, cut a small hole in it, leaving a flap to be closed after it is filled with treats. Tape the flap closed with masking tape and add more tissue if necessary.

(Left) No children's party in Santa Fe would be complete without the breaking of a piñata! Photograph © by Joe Maggiore.

(Below) Desiree and Sonja Roybal of San Ildefonso Pueblo. Courtesy of The Shop, West San Francisco, Santa Fe. Photograph © by Marcia Keegan.

Storing Holiday Cookies

To preserve the freshness and flavor of your holiday cookies, follow these basic guidelines for storing and freezing cookies after baking:

Cool the cookies before storing. If they are still warm, they are likely to stick together.

Store the cookies unfrosted; the frosting may cause sticking. Also, cookies tend to absorb moisture from frosting and lose their crispness.

Store the crisp and soft cookies separately. Stored together, they'll all become soft.

Use tightly covered containers or sealed plastic bags for storing cookies. Either will prevent humidity from softening crisp cookies and air from drying out the soft ones.

Cookies generally freeze well up to twelve months. Use freezer bags or airtight containers.

Most cookies may be stored at room temperature for up to three days. However, any cookies with a frosting or filling that contains cream cheese or yogurt must be refrigerated.

Mexican folkart, candles, and an antique Moroccan rug set the scene for this party. Photograph © by Joe Maggiore.

Las Posadas Party

A Santa Fe Christmas celebration wouldn't be complete without a trip to the plaza to be part of the old Spanish miracle play *Las Posadas*. It's a special night for Richard, who first gathers friends at his house, giving each guest a red woolen Christmas scarf, candle cups for the procession, and a script of *Las Posadas* (with the English translation) for those who aren't familiar with the play.

"I love the crisp cold of the night, the carolers, the scent of the burning piñon fires from fireplaces around the plaza," he said. "The appearance of the devil is my favorite. My friends and I always try for the loudest boos. Returning home, I have on hand dozens of candles ready to light and the fireplace ready to ignite. For refreshments, I serve freshly baked *Bizcochitos* and Holiday Hot Chocolate.

Menu

Bizcochitos
Holiday Hot Chocolate

Recipes

BIZCOCHITOS

*1 pound lard (although the traditional recipes
    call for lard, health-conscious cooks may
    substitute vegetable shortening)*

1 cup sugar

2 eggs

2 teaspoons aniseed

6 cups flour

3 teaspoons baking powder

1 teaspoon salt

½ cup sugar and 1 teaspoon cinnamon, mixed well

Mix the lard or vegetable shortening and sugar until creamy. Add the eggs and the aniseed and cream some more. Sift the flour with the baking powder and salt and mix with the first mixture. Add enough water to hold the dough together. Roll out the dough ¼ inch thick on a floured board and cut it into Christmas shapes with cookie cutters. Sprinkle with the sugar and cinnamon mixture. Bake in a 375-degree oven 10 to 12 minutes. Makes 6 dozen.

HOLIDAY HOT CHOCOLATE

½ cup sugar

¼ cup cocoa powder

1½ cups cold water

1 teaspoon ground cinnamon

¾ teaspoon ground cloves

6 cups milk

2 tablespoons vanilla

Combine the sugar, cocoa, water, cinnamon, and cloves. Mix and simmer for 5 minutes. Slowly add the milk and heat until just scalded. Do not boil. Stir continually until smooth. Mix in the vanilla and serve. Serves 6.

Santa Fe Plaza. Photograph © by Scott Christopher.

(Above) Canyon Road, once a prehistoric Indian trade route, is now a chic, gallery-lined mecca for Christmas shoppers and year-round art collectors. On Christmas Eve it embodies the spirit of a Santa Fe Christmas. Photograph © by Eduardo Fuss.

(Right) A blending of Spanish antiques, colorful Mexican pottery, and banks of poinsettias provide the centerpiece for a spectacular Christmas Eve Midnight Buffet. Photograph © by Joe Maggiore.

Christmas Eve Midnight Buffet

La Buena Noche, Christmas Eve, is probably the most magical night of the year in Santa Fe. Residents and visitors alike fill the ancient plaza, attend gallery and private parties, stroll down famed Canyon Road, and attend Midnight Mass at St. Francis Cathedral. For Richard, the evening marks the end of weeks of preparation and anticipation.

"Christmas Eve in Santa Fe is truly unforgettable," he said. "There's a timeless wonder about it that makes me feel like a little boy again. The entire town is aglow with lights—little white ones twinkling in trees and, of course, thousands of *farolitos*. To me, the highlight of the evening is to walk down Canyon Road, stopping at favorite art galleries for a visit and glass of cider or wine, singing Christmas carols around blazing *luminarias*, and enjoying the wonderful atmosphere of peace and goodwill. It's an experience that truly brings people from all walks of life together.

"Afterwards, I enjoy having friends over for an informal Christmas Eve Midnight Buffet. It's a wonderful way to end the evening and requires a minimum of effort because everything on the menu can be prepared in advance."

Canyon Road

If streets could talk, Canyon Road would have plenty of tales to tell. Called El Camino del Canon by early Spanish settlers, the narrow, winding road was once little more than a burro trail. Today, it attracts art collectors, shoppers, and sightseers from around the world.

Centuries-old adobe buildings are crowded close together, jutting out almost into the street. At one time the buildings were all private homes; however, in recent years most of them have been converted into art galleries, boutiques, and restau-

Music fills the air as Christmas Eve carolers gather around luminarias *(bonfires) along Canyon Road. Photograph © by Jim Gautier.*

rants. Called "the art and soul of Santa Fe," Canyon Road does a lively, year-round business.

On Christmas Eve, however, Canyon Road provides the setting for pure holiday magic and festive parties. For much of the evening, automobile traffic is blocked off. Galleries, shops, and homes glow with the light of thousands of *farolitos*. It's a night to remember as locals and tourists alike gather around *luminarias* to warm themselves, exchange greetings, and sing Christmas carols.

Farolitos and Luminarias

Christmas in Santa Fe is practically synonymous with lights—hundreds of thousands of them—flickering on rooftops and lining walkways. Called *farolitos*, the "little lanterns" are made from ordinary brown paper bags, sand, and candles. These glowing holiday decorations cast a special magic over the ancient city.

Farolitos are not to be confused with *luminarias*, little bonfires that symbolically light the way for the coming of the Christ Child. According to legend, this custom dates back to the three shepherds who welcomed the birth of Jesus. Bonfires were certainly common during biblical times as a practical way for shepherds to ward off the cold and protect their flocks of sheep from wolves and thieves.

The first recorded connection of *luminarias* with a Christmas Eve celebration in the New World occurred in 1536 when Mexican Indians were encouraged by Franciscan monks to light bonfires in honor of the birth of Christ. The custom was later brought to New Mexico by Spanish colonists.

The idea for *farolitos* possibly came from delicate paper lanterns made in China and imported to Mexico. Not until cheap brown paper bags became available in the late 1800s, however, was the custom adopted in Santa Fe. Now Christmas wouldn't be Christmas in the City Different without the romantic holiday atmosphere they provide.

Menu

White Sangria
Grilled Jalapeño Chiles Stuffed
with Goat Cheese
Pickled Shrimp on Skewers
Pinto Bean Bruschetta
Holiday Tortilla Stew
Blue Corn Bread Sticks
Tropical Fruit Platter
with Orange-Mango Sauce
Sopaipillas (page 27)

Recipes

WHITE SANGRIA

1 cup sugar

2 bottles good dry white wine

2 cups Spanish brandy (or other full brandy)

6 cups gingerale

3 whole cinnamon sticks

24 cloves

2 red delicious apples, cut into cubes

1 orange, cut into slices

Dissolve the sugar in water in a large pitcher. Add the wine, brandy, gingerale, spices, and fruit. Refrigerate 1 to 2 hours. Add ice cubes and serve with some of the fruit. Serves 6 to 8.

GRILLED JALAPEÑO CHILES STUFFED WITH GOAT CHEESE

12 jalapeño chiles (a milder variety, such as poblano, New Mexico, or Anaheim chiles may be substituted)

2 tablespoons roasted red bell peppers, minced (page 57)

½ cup goat cheese

2 tablespoons olive oil

Slit the chiles down one side to the end. Gently pull them apart and scrape out all the seeds. Press the red bell peppers into the goat cheese. Don't overmix. Fill the chiles and press them closed. Brush them with olive oil and grill them for 5 minutes, turning often. Serves 6.

(Opposite page) Courtesy of Nedra Matteucci's Fenn Galleries. Photograph © by Eduardo Fuss.

(Pages 78–79) Brass Mexican lanterns light the way to a table of tempting hors d'oeuvres and White Sangria. Photograph © by Joe Maggiore.

PICKLED SHRIMP ON SKEWERS

6 large yellow onions, sliced thin

1 quart kosher whole dill pickles

2 quarts white vinegar

1 quart light Wesson oil or canola oil

1 pint lemon juice

½ cup Worcestershire sauce

1 jar pickling spices

½ lemon, sliced

5 pounds large shrimp, deveined and cooked

16 whole jalapeño *chiles and 2 lemons,*

cut into small wedges, to add to skewers

8-inch bamboo skewers

Slice the onions, chop the pickles in a food processor, and mix all the ingredients together except the lemon slices, shrimp, chiles, and lemon wedges. In a tall jar with a lid, layer lemon slices and shrimp in the pickling marinade. Allow shrimp to marinate for 2 to 3 days in the refrigerator. Place the pickled shrimp on wooden skewers alternating shrimp with *jalapeño* chiles and lemon wedges. Brush with marinade and serve. This recipe will keep for weeks in the refrigerator. Serves 18 to 24.

PINTO BEAN BRUSCHETTA

1 cup freshly cooked pinto beans or

1 can drained pinto beans

1 pound plum tomatoes

5 tablespoons extra virgin olive oil

1 teaspoon ground cumin

½ teaspoon dry chile flakes

2 cloves garlic, minced

2 teaspoons balsamic vinegar

3 teaspoons chopped fresh cilantro

Salt and pepper to taste

1 loaf Italian bread, cut into rounds

To cook the beans, soak them overnight in water. Drain and rinse the beans. Cover the beans with fresh water in a large pot. Boil briskly for 15 minutes. Drain and cover the beans with fresh water. Then cook, uncovered, for 1 hour or until tender.

When the beans have been cooked, drain them. Dice the tomatoes. Place them in a strainer and sprinkle them with salt. Let them drain 15 to 20 minutes.

In a bowl mix the beans, 4 tablespoons of the olive oil, cumin, chile flakes, garlic, vinegar, and cilantro. Salt and pepper to taste.

Brush the bread rounds with the remaining olive oil. Place them on a baking sheet and broil them 5 to 6 minutes until crisp and lightly brown. Spoon the bean mixture onto the toasted bread rounds and serve. Makes 24.

Note: Bean mixture can be made 1 to 2 hours ahead and kept at room temperature.

HOLIDAY TORTILLA STEW

3 cups chicken breast, shredded

2 Anaheim chiles

1 red bell pepper

2 ears yellow corn, or substitute 1 package

frozen corn

4 large tomatoes

1 pound chorizo, *sautéed and drained*

2 strips lean bacon, chopped

2 medium onions, chopped

2 teaspoons fresh oregano or 1 teaspoon dried

1½ teaspoons ground cumin

4 cloves garlic, crushed

6 cups fresh chicken stock (page 95)

Salt and pepper to taste

4 cups zucchini, diced

12 corn tortillas

1 cup vegetable oil

Fresh cilantro

Juice of 2 limes

1 cup sour cream (optional)

Grill or broil the chicken, chiles, bell pepper, and corn until blistered on all sides. Remove the skins and seeds from the chiles (use rubber gloves) and bell pepper. Coarsely chop. Cut the kernels of corn off the cobs. Parboil the tomatoes to remove the skins, chop coarsely, and set them aside.

Sauté the *chorizo* and drain off and discard all the fat. In a Dutch oven or large pot fry the bacon until crisp; then remove and chop it, saving the

drippings. Add the chopped onions to the bacon drippings and sauté them until they are clear, 3 to 5 minutes.

Add the tomatoes, chicken, *chorizo*, oregano, cumin, garlic, and chicken stock. Bring to a boil. Reduce the heat to a simmer. Salt and pepper to taste.

Cover and cook 20 to 30 minutes. Stir in the chopped chiles, bell pepper, corn, and zucchini and cook another 10 to 15 minutes.

Before serving, cut the corn tortillas into 1-inch strips and fry them until crisp in the vegetable oil. Drain on paper towels. Ladle the stew into bowls and garnish the bowls with tortilla chips, fresh cilantro, and lime juice.

If desired, dollop sour cream on top. Or ladle the stew into bowls and let guests add their own garnishes. Serves 12.

BLUE CORN BREAD STICKS

1 tablespoon corn oil

1 cup blue cornmeal

1 cup all-purpose flour

1 tablespoon baking powder

1/2 teaspoon salt

1 cup milk

2 eggs, lightly beaten

1/4 cup molasses

1/4 cup unsalted butter, melted

Preheat the oven to 375 degrees. Preheat a cast-iron corn mold pan (available in cook stores) in the oven for 20 minutes. Brush the inside of the molds with corn oil. Combine the dry ingredients in a medium-sized mixing bowl. Stir in the milk, eggs, molasses, and butter. Mix until blended. Spoon the batter into the greased pan, filling molds ¾ full. Bake 12 to 15 minutes or until golden brown. Serves 6.

Tasty Holiday Tortilla Stew served with hot Blue Corn Bread Sticks is always a hit with Christmas Eve guests. Photograph © by Joe Maggiore.

TROPICAL FRUIT PLATTER

1 medium pineapple, peeled, cut in half, and
  cross-cut into ¼-inch slices

1 large firm ripe papaya, peeled, halved lengthwise,
  and seeded

4 star fruit, washed and sliced into stars

4 kiwi fruit, peeled and cut into ¼-inch slices

2 medium mangos, peeled, seeded, and cut into cubes

⅓ cup pistachio nuts, coarsely chopped

1 pomegranate, broken up, seeds removed
  and reserved

ORANGE-MANGO SAUCE

½ cup orange juice

2 tablespoons honey

1 cup mango, peeled and cubed

2 tablespoons light rum

2 tablespoons brown sugar

Blend the sauce in a blender until it is smooth. Arrange the fruit on a platter. Drizzle Orange-Mango Sauce over the fruit. Sprinkle the nuts and pomegranate seeds on top and serve. Serves 6 to 8.

(Above) A Tropical Fruit Platter and Sopaipillas *provide the perfect ending to this festive meal. Photograph © by Joe Maggiore.*

*(Opposite page) * Reprinted from* La Herencia del Norte, *Winter 1994. Photograph © by Eduardo Fuss.*

La Buena Noche*

'Twas the night before Christmas and all through the *casa*
Ni un raton se movia. Caramba! Que pasa?
Los niños were all tucked away *en sus camas,*
Some in long underwear, some in *pijamas.*
While mama worked late in her little *cocina*
El viejo was down at the corner *cantina*
Living it up with *amigos, carrajo!*
Muy contento y un poco borracho.
While hanging the stockings with *mucho cuidado,*
In hopes that old Santa would feel *obligado*
To bring *a los niños* both *buenos y malos,*
A nice batch of *dulces y otros regalos.*
Outside in the yard there arose such a *grito*
That I jumped to my feet like a frightened *cabrito.*
I ran to the window *y mire afuera*
And who in the world do you think that it *era?*
St. Nick in a sleigh and a big red *sombrero*
Came dashing along like a crazy *bombero!*
And pulling his sleigh, instead of *venados,*
Were eight little burros, approaching *volados.*
I watched as they came and this quaint little *hombre*
Was shouting and whistling and calling by *nombre:*
Ay Pancho! Ay Pepe! Ay Cuca! Ay Beto!
Ay Chato! Ay Chopo! Ay Maruca y Nieta!
Then standing erect with hand *en su pecho*
He flew to the top of our very own *techo*
With his round little belly like a bowl of *jalea*
He struggled to squeeze down our old *chimenea.*
Then huffing and puffing, at last in our *sala,*
With soot smeared all over his *traje de gala,*
He filled all the stockings with *bonitos regalos*
For none of the *niños* had been *muy malos.*
Then chuckling aloud, seeming *muy contento,*
He turned like a flash *y volo como el viento.*
And I heard him exclaim *y es la verdad!*
"Merry Christmas *a todos, Feliz Navidad!*"

— Anonymous

Christmas Morning Cowboy Breakfast

On Christmas morning, Richard likes to serve an old-fashioned, ranch-style cowboy breakfast. "My recipes are variations on old family favorites," he said. "On my father's side, I'm descended from generations of northern California cattle ranchers whose land was acquired through a Mexican land grant. I guess that explains my fondness for an authentic stick-to-your-ribs Christmas breakfast."

Richard finds that guests enjoy participating in some aspect of the meal preparation. "Just before my breakfast guests arrive, I heat antique branding irons in the fireplace," he said. "Then, after serving Bloody Marys made with my special Chile Pepper Vodka, I invite guests to participate in branding batches of freshly baked tortillas.

"After breakfast, we all gather around the Christmas tree. Before we open presents, however, everyone looks for the special chile ornament that I've hidden somewhere on the tree the night before. It's my southwestern adaptation of the old European folk tradition of hiding a 'lucky' pickle ornament in the tree. In my home in Santa Fe, whoever finds the chile ornament receives an extra gift!"

Recipes

CHILE PEPPER VODKA

Place small red chiles on a bamboo skewer and set in vodka. Store in a dark cool place for 1 week.

Menu

*Bunkhouse Bloody Marys
Made with Chile Pepper Vodka
Michael's Huevos Rancheros
Served with Flour Tortillas, Spicy
Red Salsa (page 55), and
Tomatillo Salsa (page 63)
Cornmeal Crusted Trout with Bacon
Apple-Cranberry Crisp*

BUNKHOUSE BLOODY MARYS
(also delicious served without vodka)

1 shot Chile Pepper Vodka (see recipe above)
⅛ teaspoon lemon juice
Dash Worcestershire sauce
4 ounces tomato juice
Freshly ground pepper to taste
Celery stalks and red chiles for garnish

Mix the first 5 ingredients. Garnish with celery stalks and red chiles. Serves 1.

(Opposite page) Bunkhouse Bloody Marys are a tasty eye opener for a Christmas Morning Cowboy Breakfast. Photograph © by Joe Maggiore.

(Left) Photograph © by Eduardo Fuss.

MICHAEL'S HUEVOS RANCHEROS WITH RED AND GREEN CHILE SAUCE

6 white potatoes, parboiled and cut into
    ½-inch cubes

2 tablespoons olive oil

Sliced chorizo to taste

½ cup red bell pepper, diced

½ cup green chiles, diced

1 bunch green onions, chopped

12 eggs

½ cup milk

⅓ cup Bisquick®

½ cup cheddar cheese, shredded

1 teaspoon salt

½ teaspoon pepper

Fry the potatoes in the olive oil for 2 to 3 minutes. Add the *chorizo*, bell pepper, chiles, and onions, and cook 15 to 20 minutes longer. Stir gently to avoid breaking up the potatoes.

In a medium-sized bowl mix the eggs, milk, Bisquick, cheese, salt, and pepper. Whisk with a fork until the ingredients are blended. Add to the potato mixture and cook over a medium heat until the eggs are set, approximately 5 to 8 minutes. Serve with fresh hot flour tortillas and side dishes of Spicy Red Salsa (page 55) and *Tomatillo* Salsa (page 63). Serves 4 to 6.

CORNMEAL CRUSTED TROUT WITH BACON

3 strips bacon

1 teaspoon mixed dry herbs (bouquet garni)

1 teaspoon salt

1 cup yellow cornmeal

4 fresh trout

1 cup buttermilk

¼ cup clarified butter

Lemon wedges and fresh cilantro for garnish

Fry the bacon until crisp and brown in a large nonstick pan, about 15 minutes. Drain on paper towels.

Mix the herbs and salt with the cornmeal. Rinse the trout and pat dry. Dip the trout in the buttermilk then into the cornmeal-herb mixture.

Add the butter to the bacon drippings in the frying pan and fry the trout over high heat about 6 minutes on each side, turning carefully, until golden brown. The trout should be moist and tender. Crumble the bacon on top and garnish with lemon wedges and cilantro. Serves 4.

FLOUR TORTILLAS

2 cups all-purpose flour

½ teaspoon baking powder

1 teaspoon salt

3 tablespoons lard, or substitute vegetable shortening

½ cup lukewarm water

Mix the dry ingredients in a bowl. Work in the lard or vegetable shortening. Add the water and mix well. Turn the dough out on a floured board and knead it for 5 to 8 minutes or until it feels elastic. Cover and let stand for about 30 minutes.

Divide the dough into small 1½-inch balls. Roll them out to about 6 to 8 inches in diameter. Cook the tortillas on a hot, ungreased griddle until lightly browned on both sides but still soft and supple. Makes 10 to 12.

Note: To add a special cowboy touch to the tortillas, Richard heats an antique branding iron in the fireplace and invites guests to help brand the tortillas.

APPLE-CRANBERRY CRISP

Crisp

½ cup flour

½ cup brown sugar

1 teaspoon ginger

1 teaspoon nutmeg

½ cup walnuts, chopped

4 tablespoons butter

Filling

8 large Granny Smith apples, peeled, cored, and diced

2 cups fresh cranberries, washed and picked over

½ cup packed brown sugar

½ cup granulated sugar

1 teaspoon ground ginger

1 teaspoon ground nutmeg

¼ cup apple cider

Crisp: In a medium-sized bowl combine the flour, brown sugar, ginger, nutmeg, and chopped walnuts. Mix thoroughly by hand. Add the butter slowly and mix with your fingers until the mixture forms large coarse crumbs. Preheat the oven to 375 degrees.

Filling: In a large bowl, toss the apples and cranberries with the brown sugar, granulated sugar, ginger, and nutmeg. Drizzle apple cider over the mixture.

Spoon the mixture into a buttered 12 x 12-inch baking pan. Spread the crisp on top and bake for 1 hour or until golden brown. Serves 4 to 6.

(Above) Apple-Cranberry Crisp and freshly brewed coffee. Photograph © by Joe Maggiore.

(Below) Ranch house porch. Photograph © by Scott Christopher.

(Pages 88–89) A spectacular holiday setting with a selection of crafts, tableware, and decorations, including hammered Mexican brass, Spanish glass, festive dinnerware, decorated favors, folk animals, candles, poinsettias, and Christmas cactus. Photograph © by Joe Maggiore.

Richard believes that every social occasion should be enhanced with a beautiful table setting. A festive effect is created by these serape-colored napkins, brightly patterned plates, and multishaded beads. Photograph © by Joe Maggiore.

A Santa Fe Christmas Dinner

The most unforgettable Christmas parties contain an element of surprise, according to Richard. "The trick is to combine traditional holiday activities and recipes with the unexpected," he said. "I try to keep the surprises coming."

To begin, arriving guests are invited to gather by the piano for Christmas singing, which helps to establish a relaxed party mood.

The fiesta atmosphere continues at the dinner table, as guests open decorated cardboard favors containing paper hats, Guatemalan worry dolls, fortunes, and treats. "Within five minutes everyone is laughing and having a wonderful time," Richard said.

"This has been part of my Christmas dinner for years. Imagine a table full of adults wearing silly paper hats while eating an elegant meal! It's the unexpected that makes any party really special."

Recipes

MARGARITAS

1½ tablespoons superfine sugar

1 ounce fresh lime juice

1½ ounces tequila

1 ounce triple sec or other orange-flavored liqueur

Lime wedges for garnish

Mix the ingredients and shake with ice (or blend in a blender with ice for frozen Margaritas). Strain into a chilled glass with salted rim. Garnish with a lime wedge. Serves 1.

Menu

Margaritas
Spanish-style Almonds with Sea Salt
Mini-Tamales with Tomatillo Salsa
Garlic Olives
Mussels on Saffron Rice
Grilled Skewered Pork and Vegetables
Richard's Red Hot Hens
Red Hot Hen Stuffing
Mom's Cranberry-Orange Relish
Roasted Pepper-Corn Relish
Papaya-Cactus Pad Salad
with Poppy Seed Dressing
Roasted Garlic Mashed Potatoes
Southwestern Green Beans
Jalapeño Corn Muffins
Piñon Nut Torte
Spanish Coffee (page 65)

Whole roasted heads of garlic give an exciting flavor to Richard's Roasted Garlic Mashed Potatoes. Photograph © by Joe Maggiore.

SPANISH-STYLE ALMONDS WITH SEA SALT

½ pound raw almonds

1 teaspoon olive oil

1 tablespoon coarse kosher sea salt

Place the almonds in a saucepan. Cover them with water and bring them to a rapid boil for 3 minutes. Rinse in cold water and remove the skins. Sauté the nuts in the olive oil, stirring the pan continually until the almonds are an even light golden color. Drain on paper towels and sprinkle with the salt. Serve warm. Makes 1½ cups.

MINI-TAMALES WITH TOMATILLO SALSA

¼ cup yellow onions, minced

2 tablespoons olive oil

3 cups Masa Harina

1 cup vegetable shortening

2 eggs, beaten

½ teaspoon salt

½ teaspoon chile powder

1 tablespoon sugar

½ teaspoon ground cumin

½ teaspoon baking powder

1 cup fresh corn kernels, soaked and cut from the cob, or substitute frozen corn

¼ cup red bell pepper, minced

2 Anaheim chiles, roasted, skinned, seeded, and chopped or ¼ cup canned mild green chile

2 jalapeño chiles, seeded and chopped

18 dry corn husks, soaked in hot water until soft

3 yards natural raffia, soaked in hot water until soft

In a small skillet, sauté the onions in the olive oil for 3 to 4 minutes and set aside. Using a large bowl, combine the Masa Harina, vegetable shortening, eggs, salt, chile powder, sugar, cumin, and baking powder until well blended. Add the corn, bell pepper, chiles, and onions. Mix thoroughly.

Spread 2 heaping tablespoons of the mixture onto 5 x 5-inch trimmed and soaked corn husks. Roll the husks into a tube and tie both ends with raffia. Lay the tamales in a vegetable steamer and steam for 20 minutes. Serve with *Tomatillo* Salsa (page 63). Serves 18.

GARLIC OLIVES

1 jar large green olives

1 jar black olives with pits

1 jar red Greek olives

4 cloves garlic, crushed

12 whole black peppercorns

12 whole red peppercorns

1/4 teaspoon dried crushed red pepper flakes

3 tablespoons fresh lemon juice

1/4 cup olive oil

3 sprigs fresh rosemary

Drain and rinse the olives in a medium-sized bowl, reserving the brine. Toss the olives with the garlic, peppercorns, pepper flakes, lemon juice, and olive oil. In a large jar, layer the olive mixture with the fresh rosemary. Fill the jar with reserved olive brine and seal the lid tightly. Shake well. Let the olives marinate for 1 week in the refrigerator. Keeps up to 1 month, refrigerated. Serve drained with fresh lemon rind strips at room temperature. Makes 3 cups.

MUSSELS ON SAFFRON RICE

2/3 cup white wine

1/2 white onion, finely chopped

1 1/2 pounds mussels, scrubbed and debearded

2–2 1/2 cups chicken stock (page 95)

Pinch saffron threads

1 cup pearl rice

2–3 tablespoons minced red bell pepper

Salt and white pepper to taste

4 tablespoons extra virgin olive oil

3 garlic cloves, minced

1 tablespoon minced parsley

1/2 teaspoon grated lemon peel

3 tablespoons red wine vinegar

Juice from 1/2 lemon

Cilantro and lemon wedges for garnish

Bring the white wine to a boil in a large saucepan; then add 1/2 of the onions. Add the mussels. Cover and steam for 5 to 7 minutes, until they open. After cooling, remove the mussels, reserving the shells.

In a saucepan, bring the chicken stock to a boil. Add the saffron threads and rice, bring back to a boil, and cook until most of the liquid is absorbed. Add the minced red bell pepper. Lower the heat and simmer until the remaining liquid is absorbed. Salt and pepper to taste.

In a large skillet, heat the olive oil and sauté the remaining onions and garlic for 2 minutes, but do not let them brown. Add the parsley, stir, and remove from the heat. Add the mussels, lemon peel, and wine vinegar. Cover and refrigerate for 1 hour. With a slotted spoon, mound the slightly warm rice on half mussel shells. Top each shell with 1 mussel and a squeeze of lemon juice. Garnish with fresh cilantro and lemon wedges. Serves 4 to 6.

GRILLED SKEWERED PORK AND VEGETABLES

16 8-inch bamboo skewers

3 tablespoons olive oil

Juice of 1 lime

2 teaspoons garlic, minced

1 tablespoon onion, minced

3 tablespoons red wine vinegar

2 tablespoons chopped cilantro

1 pound pork loin, cubed

16 cherry tomatoes

16 small green chiles

8 artichoke hearts, trimmed and quartered

1 small red onion, cut into chunks

Soak the bamboo skewers overnight to avoid burning. Mix together the olive oil, lime juice, garlic, onion, vinegar, and cilantro. Marinate the pork in the mixture for 1 to 3 hours. Skewer the ingredients in the following order: 1 tomato, chile,

artichoke heart, marinated pork cube, and piece of red onion. Grill for 5 to 7 minutes, turning after 3 minutes on each side. Baste with the marinade sauce while grilling. Makes 16.

RICHARD'S RED HOT HENS

4 Cornish game hens

Salt and pepper

1/3 cup red currant jelly

1 tablespoon honey

2 1/2 tablespoons crushed red chile flakes

1 tablespoon dry sherry

Remove the giblets from the game hens. Rinse and pat dry. Salt and pepper inside of the hens and place them in a shallow roasting pan, breast side up.

Preheat the oven to 400 degrees. Mix the jelly, honey, chile flakes, and sherry until smooth. Then simmer over low heat until bubbly. Baste the hens. Set them in the lower third of the oven for the first 20 minutes. Reduce the temperature to 350 degrees and continue roasting the birds another 40 minutes, basting about every 15 minutes or until golden brown and the juice runs clear from the thigh

when pierced. Let the hens stand 5 minutes before serving. Serves 4.

Note: This glaze also works well with turkeys.

RED HOT HEN STUFFING

1 9 x 13-inch pan of baked corn bread

2 pounds chorizo (casings removed), cooked and drained

2 teaspoons ground cumin

1/4 cup vegetable oil

2 medium yellow onions, chopped

2 red bell peppers, chopped

2 large stalks celery, chopped

1 teaspoon fresh oregano

Salt and pepper to taste

2 8-ounce cans chopped green chiles

3 cups fresh chicken stock (page 95)

1 1/2 cups walnuts, chopped

1/2 cup fresh parsley, chopped

1/2 cup butter, melted

2 large eggs, beaten

1/2 stick cold butter

Crumble the corn bread and *chorizo* together in a large mixing bowl. Add the cumin. Heat the vegetable oil over low heat and add the onions, bell peppers, celery, oregano, salt, and pepper to taste. Cover and cook 5 or 6 minutes until the vegetables are wilted. Combine with the sausage mixture. Add the green chiles, chicken stock, walnuts, parsley, butter, and eggs. Mix well and press into a buttered loaf pan. Dot with the cold butter, cover with foil, and bake for 1 hour at 350 degrees. Serves 6.

CHICKEN STOCK

1–3 tablespoons olive oil

2 large carrots, peeled and cut into chunks

3 celery stalks, cut up

2 large yellow onions, cut into chunks

1 tablespoon white peppercorns

½ cup parsley tips, coarsely chopped

4 whole bay leaves

8 cloves garlic, minced

1 turnip, coarsely cut

1 parsnip, coarsely cut

6 teaspoons powdered chicken stock or
   1 tablespoon salt

5 pounds chicken bones (backs, necks, and wing tips)

1 gallon water

In a large stockpot, heat the oil and add all the ingredients except the chicken and water. Cover and sauté at high heat, stirring frequently for 5 to 8 minutes. Add the chicken and water. Bring to a boil. Remove the scum with a spoon. Lower the heat and simmer, uncovered, for 4 hours. Strain, let cool, refrigerate, and skim off any remaining fat. Makes 3 quarts.

Note: Stock freezes well.

CORN HUSK FRILLS FOR HEN'S LEGS

While the hens are baking, soak 6 natural corn husks in warm water for 20 to 30 minutes. For each hen, cut 2 corn husks into 4½ x 3-inch rectangles. Fold in half crosswise. From the folded center, cut ¾ of the way into the corn husks. Repeat, making a frill across each corn husk. The cuts should be ¼ inch apart. Set the corn husks aside

in warm water until the hens are done. When the hens are out of the oven, wrap the folded corn husks around the legs and tie with raffia. Fluff the ends. Serve the hens on a bed of stuffing with Mom's Cranberry-Orange Relish (see below).

MOM'S CRANBERRY-ORANGE RELISH

2 medium red apples, unpeeled and cut into eighths

½ cup sugar

2 whole seedless oranges, unpeeled and
   cut into eighths

1 pound fresh cranberries, washed

¼ jar jalapeño chile jelly (optional)

3 oranges, halved (optional)

Using a food processor fitted with a steel blade, finely chop the apples a few at a time. Mix in the sugar. Mix in the oranges, then the cranberries. Process only until coarse, not mushy. Add jelly, if desired. Chill overnight for the best flavor. Serve in orange cups. Serves 6 to 8.

To make 6 cups, hollow out the orange halves and scallop the edges in a zigzag design. Fill with the relish.

ROASTED PEPPER-CORN RELISH

2½ teaspoons Thai Hot Pepper Sauce
   (available in supermarkets)

¼ cup apple cider vinegar

3 tablespoons honey

1 teaspoon ground turmeric

1 teaspoon salt

⅓ cup olive oil

2 10-ounce packages frozen corn kernels,
   thawed and drained

1 roasted red bell pepper, skinned,
   seeded, and chopped (see directions, page 57)

½ cup chopped red onions

¼ cup chopped cilantro

In a large bowl, combine the Thai Hot Pepper Sauce, vinegar, honey, turmeric, and salt. Slowly whisk in the olive oil. Add the corn, red bell pepper, red onions, and cilantro. Refrigerate overnight, stirring occasionally. Bring to room temperature before serving. Serves 6 to 8.

Richard's signature table setting teams this colorful contemporary southwestern china pattern with Mexican pottery and serape-patterned napkins and place mats. In addition, his tapas look as good as they taste. Photograph © by Joe Maggiore.

PAPAYA-CACTUS PAD SALAD WITH POPPY SEED DRESSING

¹/₃ cup slivered almonds

1 tablespoon butter

1 head romaine lettuce, torn into bite-sized pieces

1 head red leaf lettuce, torn into bite-sized pieces

1 firm, ripe papaya, peeled, seeded, and cubed

1 ruby red grapefruit, peeled and sectioned

2 fresh cactus pads, scrubbed and scraped of needles

Sauté the almonds in the butter, turning often, until golden brown. Drain on paper towels. Dice 1 cactus pad. Combine all the ingredients except for the almonds and 1 cactus pad. Toss the salad with Poppy Seed Dressing. Decorate with the remaining cactus pad (see directions below). Sprinkle with the almonds and serve. Serves 4 to 6.

Cactus Pad Decoration: After the salad is assembled and tossed, poke a 6-inch bamboo skewer into the bottom of the remaining cactus pad. Snip off a 1-inch piece of another skewer and poke it into a Christmas cactus flower or another small flower and insert the flower into the side of the cactus. Stand the cactus pad upright in the salad.

POPPY SEED DRESSING

¹/₄ cup fresh orange juice

¹/₄ cup olive oil

2 teaspoons poppy seeds

1¹/₂ teaspoons orange peel, finely shredded

¹/₄ teaspoon salt

1 teaspoon honey

Combine all the ingredients in a screw-top jar and shake well. Chill for 1 hour. Makes ½ cup.

ROASTED GARLIC MASHED POTATOES

2 whole garlic heads

Olive oil

4 pounds russet potatoes

¹/₂ stick butter

¹/₄ cup Parmesan cheese

¹/₂ cup half-and-half

Salt and pepper to taste

Remove the tops from the garlic heads and brush them with olive oil. Place on foil upright in a baking pan and bake in a 400-degree oven for 45 minutes or until caramelized and golden brown inside.

Peel the potatoes and quarter. Cover them with water and bring to a boil, covered. Cook until they are very tender (a knife should easily pass through them). Drain.

Press garlic paste from the skins and add. Remove any remaining skins. Add the butter, cheese, and half-and-half and mash until smooth. Salt and pepper to taste. Serves 4 to 6.

SOUTHWESTERN GREEN BEANS

2 pounds green beans

¹/₂ stick butter

6 Anaheim chiles, roasted (page 57)

1 red bell pepper, roasted (page 57)

¹/₄ teaspoon ground cumin

Salt and pepper to taste

Wash and trim the string beans. In a heavy saucepan, bring the beans to a boil and cook until tender (about 5 minutes). Drain the water. Melt the butter in a frying pan and add the chiles, roasted red bell pepper, cumin, and green beans. Coat evenly for about 5 minutes. Salt and pepper to taste. Serves 4 to 6.

JALAPEÑO CORN MUFFINS

3 strips bacon

2 ears corn, shucked, or substitute 1 cup frozen corn

1¹/₂ cups blue or yellow cornmeal

1 cup all-purpose flour

³/₄ teaspoon salt

2 teaspoons sugar

1 teaspoon ground cumin

1 teaspoon chile powder

1 tablespoon double-acting baking powder

2 eggs, beaten

1¹/₄ cups lowfat buttermilk

Turn a salad into a masterpiece. Richard's artful touch is apparent in this Papaya-Cactus Pad Salad with Poppy Seed Dressing. Photograph © by Joe Maggiore.

½ large cup red bell pepper, seeded,
  stemmed, and finely chopped
¼ cup jalapeño chiles, seeded, stemmed,
  and finely chopped
1 cup sharp cheddar cheese
6 dry corn husks, soaked in warm water
  and cut into ½-inch strips

Preheat the oven to 400 degrees. Fry the bacon until crisp. Cut the corn kernels off the cobs with a serrated knife. Sift together the cornmeal, flour, salt, sugar, cumin, chile powder, and baking powder in a large bowl. Beat in eggs and buttermilk until combined. Stir in the corn, bell pepper, *jalapeño* chiles, and bacon. The batter should be a little lumpy. Fold in the cheese and spoon the batter into a well-buttered muffin pan. Line the pan with criss-crossed corn husk strips for added pizzazz. Bake until golden and a toothpick inserted in the center comes out clean, about 25 minutes. Makes 1 dozen.

PIÑON NUT TORTE

Crust

1¼ cups all-purpose flour
1½ teaspoons sugar
¼ teaspoon salt
1 tablespoon grated orange peel
½ cup chilled solid vegetable shortening,
  butter flavored, cut into small pieces
2 tablespoons ice water

In a food processor combine the flour, sugar, salt, and grated orange peel. Turning the food processor on and off, cut in the vegetable shortening until coarsely blended. Add enough ice water to form moist clumps. Mold the dough into a ball; then flatten it into a disk. Wrap it in plastic wrap and refrigerate for 1 hour.

Bring the dough to room temperature and roll it out on a lightly floured surface to a size that will cover the torte pan (about 12 inches). Press the dough into the pan with your fingers and trim the edges. Place the crust in the freezer for 15 minutes. Pour in the filling and bake.

Note: A frozen pie crust works well if you need to save time.

Filling

1 cup light corn syrup
3 whole eggs, lightly beaten
⅔ cup granulated sugar
2 tablespoons butter, melted
1 teaspoon vanilla
2 cups piñon nuts, roasted

Preheat the oven to 350 degrees. Combine the corn syrup, eggs, sugar, melted butter, and vanilla in a medium-sized bowl. Whisk until the mixture is well blended and fold in the piñon nuts. Pour the filling into the torte shell and bake for about 1 hour.

Let it cool completely. Cut into wedges and serve with vanilla ice cream with candied orange strips (available at most candy stores) and Spanish Coffee (page 65). Serves 6 to 8.

Roasting Piñon Nuts: Preheat the oven to 400 degrees. Spread the nuts in a single layer on a baking sheet and roast for 7 to 12 minutes, or until they are a rich golden brown. The nuts burn easily, so keep an eye on them and shake the pan occasionally to avoid scorching.

Roasted piñon nuts add a wonderful crunchy flavor to this delicious Piñon Nut Torte. Served with Spanish Coffee, it is a perfect ending to an unforgettable Christmas dinner. Photograph © by Joe Maggiore.

Making Your Own Christmas Wreaths

Richard's Christmas greetings always start at his front door. "Hanging wreaths is a holiday tradition," he said. "But traditions need not be traditional. It's much more fun to create an individualized wreath that reflects your own personal interests and tastes. Ready-made base wreaths are simple to work with. Just use your imagination and the materials you have on hand. Whether it's a wreath or a special collection of ornaments, give it your own personal touch. Holiday decorations you put together yourself will be appreciated and remembered for years to come." In this and the following chapter, Richard designs southwestern decorations with a City Different flair.

APPLE-CINNAMON WREATH

Materials:

1 14-inch wire wreath frame

18–24 clusters fresh pine (picture at right)

22-gauge florist wire

6–9 cinnamon sticks

4 yards raffia

Hot glue gun

6 pinecones

4 dried apple or orange slices (see page 103)

3 dried pomegranates

4 clusters pepperberries

1 prayer feather (optional)

Instructions: Wire fresh pine clusters onto the wire wreath frame as shown, starting on the inside. Then wire the clusters to cover the outside. Fill the center in with extra branches. Tie the cinna-mon sticks in groups of 3 with raffia. Tie the raffia into bows. Hot glue in several places. Randomly hot glue pinecones, apple or orange slices, pomegranates, and pepperberries onto wreath. A prayer feather adds a Santa Fe touch.

SANTA FE SOUVENIR WREATH

Materials:

1 14-inch straw wreath

Tacky craft glue (available at craft stores)

Hot glue gun

Assorted southwestern ornaments, postcards,

*   papier mâché chiles, dried flowers, and so forth*

Instructions: Hot glue a large item in the center of the wreath as a focal point. Then glue postcards randomly around the outside edge, covering the straw wreath. Attach other items in clusters to fill in the blank areas. Add dried flowers as accents.

(Opposite page) Richard's Apple-Cinnamon Wreath adds a festive touch to the door of Celebrations Restaurant on famed Canyon Road. Photograph © by Joe Maggiore.

(Below) The start of a beautiful Christmas decoration. Richard wires fresh greens to a metal wreath ring. Photograph © by Joe Maggiore.

(Left) Why not assemble treasured items into a souvenir wreath? (See instructions page 99.) Richard uses postcards, southwestern decorations, chiles, and dried flowers to create a personalized holiday decoration. Photograph © by Joe Maggiore.

(Below) Richard incorporates his passion for Hispanic folk art into a festive holiday wreath that doubles as a year-round Santa Fe decoration. Photograph © by Scott Christopher.

SANTA FE CHAIR WREATH

Materials:

1 18-inch wreath frame

24–36 fresh pine sprigs

9–12 pieces other fresh greens

24 dried red chiles

3 miniature Mexican chairs, or substitute
    other colorful children's toys

Hot glue gun

Ribbon

Instructions: Assemble 2 or 3 different greens, including pine, into clusters. Tie the clusters into a fan about 5 to 6 inches long. Tie the fan onto the wreath frame overlapping greens inside to outside. Fill the center with extra greens. Put chairs or toys into spaces between greens to fill and glue in place with hot glue. Add the ribbon last.

HERB-MEDICINE BAG WREATH

Materials:

22-gauge florist wire

18–24 fans of fresh bay leaves

1 14-inch wire wreath frame

Hot glue gun

4 whole garlic heads

8 shallots

4 small red onions

Assorted clusters of oregano, thyme, and sage

24 dried red chiles

12 saffron heads

4 yarrow heads

1 medicine bag

Instructions: Wire fans of bay leaves onto the wire wreath frame, inside then outside. Fill the center

(Left) Southwestern hospitality at your front door. Antique wooden doors leading into the courtyard of a Canyon Road residence provide the perfect backdrop for Richard's colorful wreath of pomegranates, pepperberries, and pinecones. Photograph © by Joe Maggiore.

(Below) Richard uses unexpected ornaments—like handpainted toy Mexican chairs—to create a festive, lighthearted holiday wreath. Photograph © Joe Maggiore.

POMEGRANATE AND CONE WREATH

Materials:

36 fresh pine clusters

1 18-inch wire wreath frame (available at craft or
    floral shops)

22-gauge florist wire

Hot glue gun

6 dry pomegranates

12 pinecones, assorted sizes

Preserved eucalyptus sprigs

Pepperberries

Assorted dry foliage

Deer moss

3 yards red Sisal ribbon or paper ribbon, # 40
    (available at craft stores)

Instructions: Wire the clusters of fresh pine to the wire frame (fill in the same as on page 99). Hot glue (in a random pattern) the pomegranates, pinecones, eucalyptus, pepperberries, and dry foliage into place, until the wreath has a full look. Fill in the bare spots with deer moss. Cut the ribbon into 12-inch pieces to form 2 loops. Tie the ends with wire. Hot glue the ribbon onto the wreath in several places.

DRYING FRUIT TO USE IN DECORATIONS AND POTPOURRI

To dry apples or oranges, slice the fruit (with skins) into ¼-inch-thick rings. Fruit may be dried by placing it on cookie sheets in the oven at 200 degrees for 5 to 6 hours. Richard prefers, however, to dry fruit in a food dehydrator, which preserves the fruit's color and aroma better than using the oven method.

Place fruit slices in a single layer on a food dehydrator tray, making certain that the pieces don't touch or overlap. Leave the fruit in the food dehydrator for 2 to 3 days. Check often. To prevent insect infestation and enhance color, you may want to spray the dried fruit with a clear acrylic sealer.

To dry apple and orange peelings to use in potpourri, scrape off the pith, lay on a screen, and air dry for 2 to 3 days.

(Left) This Herb-Medicine Bag Wreath adds a touch of holiday magic to the carved doors of this residence off Canyon Road owned by Jim and Elizabeth McGordy. The medicine bag is by Taos artist Dawn Kohorst. Photograph © by Joe Maggiore.

(Below) Deer Skull Wreath with rope and barbed wire. Photograph © by Scott Christopher.

in with extra leaves. Hot glue garlic, shallots, onions, and bunches of oregano, thyme, and sage onto the wreath. Using the hot glue gun, fill in the empty spaces with chiles, saffron, and yarrow. Attach the medicine bag to the wreath.

DEER SKULL WREATH

Materials:

2 yards rope

1 bundle old barbed wire, rolled into wreath shape

18-gauge florist wire

1 natural bleached deer skull

Hot glue gun

Fresh piñon branches and twigs

Wool blanket material (or ribbon), cut into
*   3 inch wide and 1 yard long strip*

Instructions: Wrap the rope around the barbed wire. Wire the skull onto the barbed wire wreath. Hot glue a cluster of fresh piñon branches and twigs behind the skull. Top it off with a length of blanket material or ribbon tied in a rustic bow.

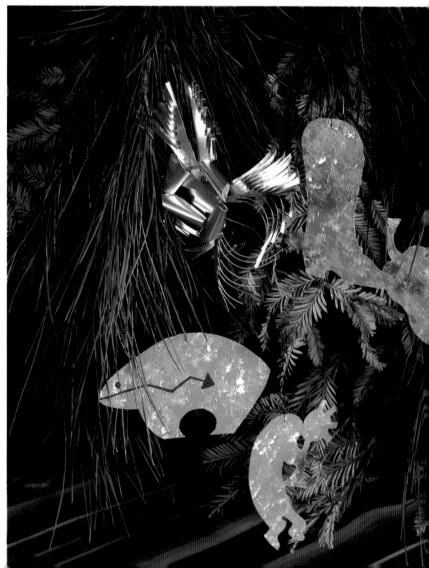

Ornaments & Decorations

"Gifts from the heart can be expressed in many different ways," according to Richard. "For crafters," he said, "this special expression comes in the giving of something handmade and one of a kind."

On the following pages, he demonstrates some

of his favorite holiday decoration and gift ideas.

SOUTHWESTERN BLANKET MITTENS AND STOCKING

Materials:

Wool blanket material

Fur or fake fur

Tacky craft glue (available at craft stores)

Small conchos

Leather strips

Instructions for mittens: Trace the pattern (page 127) onto the back of the fabric for each ornament.

Cut 2 pieces for each. Stitch the fabric backside out; then pull it inside out so that the fabric face is showing. Cut the fur trim to the desired size and glue around the top. Decorate with a concho. Glue leather strips on top for hanging.

Instructions for stocking: Trace the pattern (page 127). Follow the above directions to sew the stocking. Then, using a large needle, thread black yarn and stitch around the outside edges of the stocking. Cut fur strips to the desired size and glue around the top. Decorate with a concho. Glue leather strips on top for hanging. Now it's ready for Santa!

FIESTA ORNAMENTS

Materials: (Same materials for A and B)

Craft yarn in 4 bright colors

Tacky craft glue (available at craft stores)

Crepe paper flowers

5 3-inch Styrofoam balls (available at craft stores)

A. Ball Ornaments

Instructions: Cut the yarn into 3-foot pieces. Twist 4 colors and wrap the yarn around the balls, criss-crossing from tops to bottoms. Glue in place; then glue tassels to the bottoms. Glue paper flowers on the tops with assorted clusters of yarn and loop to the tops for hanging.

B. Tassel Ornaments

Instructions: Cut 12 strips of yarn into 10-inch pieces. Tie a piece of yarn around the center of the strips and knot. Fold the yarn once, and tie a piece of yarn around the top, 1 inch down from the first

(Opposite page, top left) Richard's Twig Cross and Dream Catcher are special gifts that will be treasured all year long (see page 106). Photograph © by Joe Maggiore.

(Opposite page, bottom left) Special Christmas ornaments and decorations like these miniature Navajo dolls by Theresa Nez can be found at Susan's Christmas Shop, located on East Palace Avenue. Owned by Susan Weber, the store does a lively business all year long. Photograph © by Joe Maggiore.

(Opposite page, upper right) Fiesta ornaments with tassels. Photograph © by Joe Maggiore.

(Opposite page, middle right) Painted natural gourd ornaments by Cathleen Kardas can also be found at Susan's Christmas Shop. Photograph © by Joe Maggiore.

(Opposite page, bottom right) Create your own Santa Fe-style Christmas tree with these easy-to-make fetish ornaments (see page 106). (Tin ornament courtesy of the Museum of New Mexico Gift Shop.) Photograph © by Joe Maggiore.

(Left) Teddy bears go southwestern when coordinated with Richard's fur-trimmed flannel gloves and stocking ornaments. Photograph © by Joe Maggiore.

knot. Trim the bottom.

TWIG CROSS

Materials:

Cardboard from a corrugated box

Brown spray paint

Assorted pine and willow twigs, ¼ inch thick

Tacky craft glue (available at craft stores)

Cone pods

String

Instructions: Cut the cardboard into a cross (see page 127 for pattern). Spray it brown. Cut the twigs and glue onto the cardboard in a pattern. Layer the contrasting twigs and glue them down. Glue the cone pods on top and fill in the center. Attach a string to the top for hanging.

DREAM CATCHER

Native American folklore speaks of magic in the night sky, the home of both good and bad dreams. Dream Catcher webs are meant to capture and hold the bad dreams, which then vanish with the morning sun, allowing only good dreams to reach the dreamer.

Materials:

1 32-inch willow branch, about ¼ inch thick

3 yards raffia

4–5 assorted feathers

Assorted beads, shells, rocks

Horsetail or doll hair (available at craft stores)

Bead wire

Instructions (see page 128): Soak the willow branch in water for 1 hour, or until pliable. Bend it into an oval frame, crisscrossing it at the top. Tie it together with a strip of raffia. To make the web, tie one end of the raffia to the willow branch. Tie 9 half hitch knots around the frame, spacing them about 1½ inches apart, keeping raffia pulled snug.

To start the next row of the web, begin tying half hitches in the middle of the raffia that is already attached. Continue tying half hitches in the same way until the opening in the center is the desired size.

To end the web, tie a double knot in the raffia and cut off the excess raffia. Make a raffia loop to hang the dream catcher. Decorate with assorted feathers, shells, rocks, strands of hair, beads, attaching them with bead wire.

SOUTHWESTERN ORNAMENTS

Materials:

Poster board

Gesso primer (available at art and craft stores)

Small natural sponge

Acrylic paint in turquoise, hunter green, and white

Small craft paintbrush (available at craft stores)

Instructions: Trace the patterns (page 127) onto white poster board and cut them out with small scissors. Brush on 2 coats of gesso, letting them dry in between. Dip the sponge into the turquoise paint and dab on the cut outs until they are completely covered with a stippling effect. Allow them to dry. Put a little white and green paint side by side. Dip the sponge into both colors and tap the sponge onto the ornaments, mixing the colors. The turquoise should show through, creating a verdigris effect. Punch a hole in the top of the ornaments with a needle and thread them for hanging.

KACHINA-STYLE ORNAMENTS

Materials:

Poster board

2 1-inch Styrofoam balls

Tacky craft glue (available at art and craft stores)

(Left) "Tree Spirits" by New Mexico artist Sheri Brown can be found at The Shop, located near the plaza on San Francisco Street. The Shop also introduced the popular Santa Fe chile lights in 1977. Photograph © by Joe Maggiore.

(Below) Apple-Chile Wreath Ornament and Annise Spice Ball.. Photograph © by Joe Maggiore.

(Below) Richard's easy-to-make Kachina-Style Ornaments are destined to become family treasures. Photograph © by Joe Maggiore.

Acrylic paints, assorted colors

Black fine line tip pen

Assorted feathers

String

Instructions: Trace *kachina* head pieces from the pattern (page 128) onto poster board and cut them out, using small scissors. Cut the Styrofoam balls in half with a serrated knife. Glue a half ball onto each cut out head piece. Coat the gesso primer over both surfaces twice, allowing them to dry in between coats. Draw the detail on the ornaments lightly with a pencil. Fill in with acrylic paints. Outline the detail with the black pen. Glue feathers to the back. Add string for a hanger.

APPLE-CHILE WREATH ORNAMENT

Materials:

18-gauge florist wire, 18 inches long

16–18 1-inch apple slices, peeled

70 bay leaves, cut into thirds

60–70 small dried red chiles, cut in half

Tacky craft glue (available at craft stores)

3 small natural pinecones

Pepperberries

Deer moss

2 yards red raffia

Instructions: Put the fresh, skinned apple slices into a food dehydrator (see page 103 for additional instructions on drying fruit). Thread 4 apple pieces, 4 bay leaves, then 4 chiles, alternating until the wire is full. Bend into a wreath and tie the ends together. Glue the pinecones, pepperberries, and deer moss over the connection. Tie a small raffia bow and glue it in the center.

ANISE SPICE BALL

Materials:

1 3-inch Styrofoam ball

Brown floral spray paint (use a craft spray
      paint that won't dissolve the Styrofoam)

1 jar star anise (available at Hispanic
      grocery stores)

Tacky craft glue (available at craft stores)

Raffia, 24 inches

1 3-inch cinnamon stick

Instructions: Spray the Styrofoam ball with spray paint until it is well covered. After the paint dries, dip the anise pods into the tacky craft glue and press them gently with the fingers onto the entire surface of the ball. The glue will dry clear. After the glue has set, tie raffia crisscrossed around the ball. Attach a cinnamon stick to the top with a small bow and a loop for hanging.

SILVERED FRUIT

Materials:

Leafing adhesive

Fresh firm fruit, such as oranges, apples, or pears

Silver metal leafing (available at craft stores)

Instructions: Brush the adhesive on the fruit in random patches. Let it dry according to instructions. Apply the leafing by pressing it onto the adhesive-brushed areas. Lightly brush off the excess leafing and arrange the Silvered Fruit in a bowl. This makes a gorgeous centerpiece to keep or to give as a gift.

Note: This fruit is no longer edible.

A feast for the eyes! Beautiful Silvered Fruit makes a wonderful gift. Photograph © by Joe Maggiore.

Keegan

Clear Light

Southwestern Gift Foods

Traditionally, Santa Feans love to celebrate Christmas. The multicultural celebration includes those things from the heart—such as warm greetings, good food prepared with love, family, and friends.

Part of the fun of Christmas for Richard is preparing special food gifts. "Flavored vinegars and oils make lovely presents," he said. "I always add a handwritten label and a recipe card to go with them."

VINEGAR IN THE NEW WORLD

So important was vinegar to survival in the New World that every colonist sailing from England was urged to include two gallons in his or her first year's food rations.

OLIVE OIL IN SPANISH COOKING

Olive oil, a key ingredient in traditional Spanish cooking, is fast gaining popularity in the United States. A few notes on storing the oil: keep it in a cool, dark place but not in the refrigerator. Store it in containers of glazed clay, very clean tin, stainless steel, or glass. Dark bottles help protect the oil from ultraviolet light.

Only premium-quality or extra virgin olive oil should be used for seasoning. Heating the oil tends to destroy the complex flavors. In addition to tossing it in salads and pastas, try brushing it over grilled foods and warm cooked vegetables. It's also delicious drizzled on grilled bread rubbed with garlic. Or simply dip freshly baked bread into little saucers of seasoned oil.

Recipes

CHILE-GARLIC HERB VINEGAR

2 chiles on a bamboo skewer

6 cloves garlic, peeled

4 sprigs fresh rosemary

1 teaspoon black peppercorns

32 ounces white vinegar

Cheesecloth

Decorative bottle

Raffia

Assorted beads, conchos, southwestern items

Sterilize a large jar with a tight lid. Place the skewered chiles, garlic, rosemary, and peppercorns in the jar. In a saucepan, heat the vinegar to a boil. Pour the vinegar into the jar over the chiles and

(Opposite page) Fresh herbs and spices steeped in olive oil and vinegar make delicious southwestern Christmas gifts. Richard displays his decorated bottles next to Zuni fetishes and pottery by Santo Domingo artist Robert Tenorio. Photograph © by Joe Maggiore.

(Below) Apple cider vinegar that has been boiled, flavored with raspberries, and strained after aging two to three weeks can be decorated and presented in an attractive gift package. Photograph © by Joe Maggiore.

CHILE-GARLIC OIL

Decorative bottle

3 large, hot red chiles on bamboo skewers

6 cloves garlic

2 large sprigs fresh rosemary

1 tablespoon black peppercorns

8 cups extra virgin olive oil

Sterilize a large decorative bottle. Add the chiles, garlic, rosemary, and peppercorns. Slowly add the olive oil and seal the bottle. Place the bottle in a cool place for 1 week to age. Decorate the bottle for holiday gift giving.

MULLING SPICE BUNDLES

¼ cup allspice

½ cup cloves

½ cup orange peel, chopped and dried (page 103)

½ cup cinnamon sticks, crushed

Cheesecloth and cotton string

Raffia, assorted beads, and southwestern items

Decorative jar

To make spice bundles, combine all spices. Place ¼ cup spices onto a square of cheesecloth and tie into a bundle with cotton string. Recipe makes 4 bundles. Put bundles in a decorative jar with a copy of the recipe for Mulled Wine (below). Seal the jar and decorate it with raffia bows, assorted beads, and southwestern items.

MULLED WINE

1 orange

8–10 whole cloves

1 mulling spice bundle

Cheesecloth and cotton string

1 bottle dry red wine

6 cups apple cider

Orange slices and cinnamon sticks

Cut the orange in half. Poke the cloves into the skin of each half. Pour the wine and apple cider into a saucepan and add orange halves and spice bundle. Simmer slowly for 30 minutes. Remove orange halves and spices. Serve with a fresh orange slice and a cinnamon stick. Serves 12 to 18.

(Left) Hearty Mulled Wine is a traditional warming treat that goes back to colonial times. For holiday gift giving, Richard prepares Mulling Spice Bundles to accompany bottles of red wine such as burgundy or Beaujolais. Photograph © by Joe Maggiore.

(Below) The holidays are a time for nourishing our souls, with good friends, good food, and good cheer. Photograph © by Joe Maggiore.

rosemary. Add the garlic and peppercorns. Allow 2 to 3 weeks to age in a cool, dark place.

Strain the vinegar through cheesecloth. Pour the strained vinegar into a decorative, sterilized bottle. Add new chiles, sprigs of rosemary, garlic cloves, and peppercorns. Decorate the bottle with raffia bows, conchos, beads, and so forth.

ROSEMARY-GARLIC HERB VINEGAR

4 sprigs fresh rosemary

2–3 sprigs fresh thyme

32 ounces white vinegar

6 cloves garlic, peeled

1 tablespoon red peppercorns

Cheesecloth

Decorative bottle

Raffia, assorted beads, conchos, southwestern items

Sterilize a large jar with a tight lid. Place the herbs in the jar. In a saucepan, heat the vinegar to a boil. Pour the vinegar into the jar over the herbs. Add the garlic and peppercorns. Allow 2 to 3 weeks to age in a cool, dark place. Strain the vinegar through cheesecloth. Pour the strained vinegar into a decorative, sterilized jar. Add new herbs, garlic, and peppercorns. Decorate the bottle with raffia bows, conchas, beads, and so forth.

GRANDMA'S PIÑON NUT BRITTLE

2 cups sugar

1 cup light corn syrup

½ cup water

2 cups piñon nuts

1 tablespoon butter

1 teaspoon baking soda

½ teaspoon vanilla

Combine the sugar, corn syrup, and water and cook until the mixture forms a hard ball in cold water. Add the nuts and butter. Cook until the nuts are brown or until the mixture forms a brittle ball in cold water. Remove from the heat. Add the baking soda and vanilla. Stir quickly until the brittle foams and the baking soda is thoroughly mixed. Spread the candy on a well-greased marble slab or large metal tray, smoothing out the edges with a fork until candy is light in color and very thin. Break it into pieces when cold. Makes 2 pounds.

MICHAEL'S BISCOTTI

8 ounces raw almonds

2½ cups flour

1 cup sugar

2–4 eggs

1 tablespoon liqueur

½ teaspoon baking soda

½ teaspoon salt

8 tablespoons cranberries or ginger

2 egg yolks, whisked with a fork

Blanch and skin the almonds. Mix all ingredients except almonds, cranberries or ginger, and egg yolks in a food processor until coarse. Add almonds, cranberries or ginger, and pulse 2 to 3 times. On a greased cookie sheet divide the dough into 3 x 8-inch rectangles about ½ inch thick. Brush with egg yolks. Bake at 375 degrees for 30 minutes or until brown. Remove and slice on an angle to desired thickness. Bake at 350 degrees for 20 more minutes. Makes 36.

ROASTED NUTS IN HONEY

1 tall decorative glass jar

2 cups mixed roasted nuts

24 ounces fireweed honey

Fill a jar with nuts. Pour the honey slowly over the nuts until the jar is filled. Seal the jar and decorate. This is wonderful served over ice cream.

SAGE HONEY

2 sprigs fresh sage

24 ounces plain honey

Mix the ingredients and set aside for 1 week. This honey is great for basting holiday turkeys.

WALNUT-DATE CHRISTMAS TREATS

48 large dates

24 whole walnuts

Powdered sugar

Pit the dates. Shell and quarter the walnuts.

This recipe for Grandma's Piñon Nut Brittle is adapted from a peanut brittle recipe that has been in Richard's family for four generations. Wrapped in cellophane and tied with a festive bow, it makes a delicious Christmas gift. Photograph © by Joe Maggiore.

Press the walnuts into the date centers where the pits would be and press the date meat over the edges. Roll in powdered sugar.

CHOCOLATE-COATED DRIED APRICOTS

12 ounces semisweet chocolate

18 ounces (4 cups) dried apricots

Melt the chocolate in a double boiler. Dip ½ of each dried apricot in chocolate and set on waxed paper to dry. Chill and pack in an airtight container.

AUNT FAYE'S HOLIDAY RING
(OR THREE KINGS BREAD)

1 cup lukewarm milk

¼ cup sugar

1 teaspoon salt

¼ cup soft shortening

1 package compressed yeast

1 egg

3¼–3½ cups flour, sifted

¼ cup softened butter or margarine

½ cup sugar mixed with 1 teaspoon cinnamon

½ cup raisins

Icing

¼ cup milk

1½ cups powdered sugar

1 tablespoon margarine

Glazed fruit and English walnuts,

   halved, for decoration

In a large bowl, mix the milk, sugar, salt, and ¼ cup shortening. Crumble the yeast into the mixture. Stir in the egg. Mix in the flour a little at a time, first using a spoon, then using your hands. Let the dough thicken until you can roll it out easily. Keep adding flour until the dough is no longer sticky and is easy to handle.

Turn the dough onto a lightly floured board. Cover and let it stand for 10 minutes to tighten up. Then knead the dough until it is smooth and elastic. Round up and set the dough to rise in a greased bowl. Cover it with a damp cloth and let it rise at 85 degrees until double in bulk, about 2 hours. Punch down the dough, round up, and set to rise again until it is not quite double in bulk, about 45 minutes.

Punch down the dough and roll it out ⅓ inch thick, into a rectangular shape about 9 x 18 inches.

Spread with the ¼ cup softened butter or margarine and sprinkle with the sugar and cinnamon mixture. Add the raisins. Roll up tightly, beginning at the wide side, and seal the edges. With the sealed edge down, transfer the roll onto a greased oblong pan or baking sheet. Join the ends to form a ring.

With scissors, make cuts ⅔ of the way through the ring at intervals of 1 inch. Turn each section on its side. Cover and let rise again until the ring is double in bulk, 35 to 40 minutes. Bake 35 to 40 minutes at 375 degrees until lightly browned.

Let cool and frost with thin icing made with milk, powdered sugar, and margarine. Frost while still warm so that the icing will run and spread well. Decorate with glazed fruit and walnuts. Serves 8.

NANNA'S ROCKY ROAD CANDY

1 pound milk chocolate

¼ pound cocoa butter

32 ounces olive oil

2 small packages marshmallows

1½ cups walnuts, chopped

Melt the chocolate and cocoa butter with the olive oil in a double boiler. Add the marshmallows, cut in half, and the walnuts. Turn the candy out onto a cool surface and let it harden. Cut into squares and store it in an airtight container. Makes 36.

JALAPEÑO CHILE JELLY

3 small cooking apples, cored, peeled, and
  coarsely chopped

8 jalapeño chiles, halved, seeded, and stemmed

1 cup chopped green sweet pepper

5 cups sugar

1½ cups cider vinegar

¼ cup water

1 6-ounce bottle liquid fruit pectin

Combine the apples, jalapeño chiles, green pepper, sugar, vinegar, and water in a Dutch oven. Bring to a rolling boil. Reduce the heat and simmer, uncovered, for 10 minutes. Strain the mixture through a sieve, pressing it with the back of a spoon to remove all the liquid. Discard the pulp.

Return the liquid to the Dutch oven and bring it to a boil. Add the pectin. Boil for 1 minute, stirring constantly. Remove the mixture from the heat. Immediately pour it into hot, sterilized pint or half-pint jars and seal.

Process in boiling water for approximately 5 minutes. Remove and cool on a wire rack. Let stand for 2 to 3 days until set. Makes 5 half-pints.

SANTA FE SEASONING MIX

2 tablespoons chile powder

2 tablespoons paprika

2 teaspoons cumin seed

2 teaspoons ground coriander

2 teaspoons sugar

2 teaspoons salt

1 teaspoon freshly ground black pepper

1 teaspoon cayenne pepper

Put all the ingredients in a blender or spice grinder and blend. Place in a pretty glass jar and store for several weeks in a cool, dry place. This is

(Left) Jalapeño Chile Jelly is all spiced up and ready for Christmas gift giving. Photograph © by Joe Maggiore.

(Below) A favorite with Richard's holiday guests, Herbed Manchego Cheese also makes a memorable holiday gift. Photograph © by Joe Maggiore.

delicious rubbed on meats or poultry before grilling. It is also good in stews, soups, or cooked vegetables.

HERBED MANCHEGO CHEESE

1 pound Manchego cheese (a semihard Spanish goat
  cheese that's mild and nutty), black rind
  removed and cut into wedges

8 cloves garlic

1 tablespoon black peppercorns

4 sprigs fresh rosemary

6 cups extra virgin olive oil

Place the cheese in a clean jar with a tight lid. Add the garlic, peppercorns, rosemary, and olive oil. Seal the jar and let the mixture age for 1 week. Remove the wedges and serve with fresh bread rounds.

Southwestern Craft Gifts

Traditions have always been important to Richard. "That's especially true at Christmas time," he said. "I get a special pleasure incorporating southwestern traditions into those of my own. That's one reason I enjoy celebrating the holidays in Santa Fe. A joyous blending of diverse cultures is really what makes this the City Different."

SOUTHWEST YULE LOG

The burning of a yule log is an ancient European custom that dates back thousands of years. Some of the ashes from the previous year were saved in the belief that using them to start the next yule fire would bring a year of good luck to the household. Why not give friends a special yule log that you have decorated, along with a handwritten note explaining the custom?

Materials:

24-inch Southwest ribbon

8 x 14-inch log

Hot glue gun

Assorted sprigs of fresh pine and greens

2 pinecones

8 dry chiles

Fireplace matches

Instructions: Cut the ribbon in half. Wrap it around the log in 2 places and glue the overlap on top. Hot glue the greens in an oval shape on the log. Glue the pinecones and chiles into the blank areas. Attach a note explaining the significance of the yule log before giving the log and the matches to someone special.

ORANGE-PEPPER POTPOURRI

Materials:

1 teaspoon ground nutmeg

3 ounces powdered orrisroot

10 drops essential oil of cinnamon

3 drops essential oil of bergamot

2 cups dried flower heads, mixed with clove heads

48 broken bay leaves

1 cup broken cinnamon sticks

4 tablespoons cloves

4 tablespoons allspice

1 cup small pinecones

1 cup dried orange peel (see instructions page 103)

(Opposite page) Two gifts in one. Richard's "Gift on a Gift" design. Photograph © by Joe Maggiore.

(Top) Richard decorates yule logs to give as special Christmas gifts. Photograph © by Joe Maggiore.

(Bottom) Not long ago, a prized gift in every child's Christmas stocking was a piece of fruit, such as a beautiful ripe orange. Although fresh fruit may not be the luxury it once was, oranges, tangerines, pears, and apples are wonderful additions to homemade potpourri and add color and charm to a traditional holiday setting. Photograph © by Joe Maggiore.

1 cup small dried red chiles

1 cup dried orange slices (page 103)

1 cup dried apple slices (page 103)

Instructions: In a bowl place the ground nutmeg, orrisroot, and essential oils. Rub them with your finger to release all the bouquet possible. Combine the remaining materials, except for some of the choicest flower heads. Mix thoroughly but gently. Place in an airtight container and store in a cool, dry place for at least 6 weeks, shaking every day or so to blend the fragrances. When arranging the potpourri, place the reserved flower heads on top for decoration.

DECORATED WINE BOTTLES

Materials:

1 3-inch twig wreath (available at craft stores)

Assorted southwestern beads, miniature skulls, chiles, feathers, leather strips, paper flowers, yarn

Tacky craft glue (available at craft stores)

Instructions: Cluster an arrangement on one side of the wreath with tacky craft glue. Layer and fill with dry material poked into the glue. The glue will dry clear. Place on a wine bottle.

DECORATED PICTURE FRAMES

Southwest Blanket Frame

Materials:

1 cardboard mat, any size (available at framing stores)

1 piece fabric, cut 1 inch longer than outside dimension of mat

Tacky craft glue (available at craft stores)

5 assorted beads

Bead wire

1 feather

Leather lacing

1 medium-sized concho

Glass, cut 1 inch larger than mat opening

Ready-made easel backing (available at framing and craft stores)

Instructions: Place the mat on the center of the fabric. Cut the center of the fabric diagonally to the

inside corner of the mat. Trim the excess fabric. Fold over the outside edge and glue to the back of the mat. Fold the fabric on the front of the mat over the edge and glue. String the beads with wire. Glue the feather onto the end of the wire and tie to the twisted leather lacing. Glue to the back of the concho. Glue the concho to the left side of the frame. Glue the glass to the opening on the back

Celebrate Christmas with a "south of the border" flavor. Colorful ornaments and wine bottle decorations add spice to your holidays. Wine courtesy of Santa Fe Vineyards Winery. Photograph © by Joe Maggiore.

side. Place a photo inside and glue the ready-made stand to the back.

Paper Frame

Instructions: Follow the directions for fabric, except substitute colored paper for material.

SANTA FE-STYLE DESK CADDY

Materials:

⅛ yard wool blanket material

Tacky craft glue (available at craft stores)

Scrap leather, 12 x 4 inches

1 willow wine basket

6 yards raffia

10–12 assorted beads

Bead wire

2 feathers

1–2 large conchos

Assorted stationery and desk accessories

Instructions: Cut the fabric into a 5 x 24-inch strip. Glue the fabric around the rim of the basket, overlapping the inside edge. Cut the leather into 1 x 12-inch strips and twist it around the basket handle, gluing the ends. Wrap the raffia around the basket to the front center and tie it into a bow. String the beads on the wire. Glue the feathers onto the ends. Knot the beads and tie them onto the bow. Glue the conchos over the bow. Twist the raffia around the handle and glue. Fill with stationery and desk accessories.

SOUTHWEST DECORATED SOAPS

Materials:

Corrugated paper

Good quality soaps

Tacky craft glue (available at craft stores)

Raffia

Bay leaves

Assorted berries and other dry materials

Instructions: Cut the paper to the size of the soaps with an extra ½-inch overlap to glue around the back. Wrap the raffia around the soaps and tie into bows. Tuck a bay leaf, colorful berries, and other dry decorative material under the raffia.

HOMEMADE BATH AND MASSAGE OILS

Stress-reducing Bath Oil

Ingredients:

4 drops essential oil of sandalwood

2 drops essential oil of jonquil

3 drops essential oil of bergamont

8 ounces almond oil

Instructions: Add the essential oils to the almond oil. Pour into a decorative bottle and let stand in a cool dark place for 1 week. Enjoy—or give as a gift.

(Top) Southwest decorated soaps are great for guests or to give as gifts to friends. Photograph © by Joe Maggiore.

(Left) Baskets and picture frames are fun and easy to decorate. Photograph © by Joe Maggiore.

Romantic Santa Fe Bath Oil

Ingredients:

6 drops essential oil of rose bulgar

3 drops essential oil of jasmine

6 freshly picked rose petals

8 ounces almond oil

Instructions: Combine the ingredients, including the rose petals. Pour into a decorative bottle and let stand in a cool dark place for 1 week.

Massage Oil

Ingredients:

10 drops essential oil of lavender

2 drops essential oil of chamomile roman

3 drops essential oil of verbena

20 ounces grape seed oil

Instructions: Combine the ingredients and pour into a decorative bottle. It is ready to use immediately.

BATH SALTS

To give bath salts as a gift, buy them in bulk and put them in decorative jars (see "Resources").

SANTA FE CANDLES

Mesa Candle

Materials:

Assorted tissue paper

1 tall votive candle in glass (available at Hispanic grocery stores)

Tacky craft glue (available at craft stores)

Instructions: Cut the paper into strips of 4 different widths. Cut scallops along the edges. Overlap the colors, starting with the widest and darkest, on the votive candle. Glue the ends in the back. Lightly brush tacky craft glue over the tissue (the glue will dry clear).

Glow Through Branches Candle

Materials:

¼-inch willow or other tree branches, trimmed

1 tall votive candle in glass (available at Hispanic grocery stores)

Hot glue gun

Raffia

Assorted dried flowers

Instructions: Cut the branches into pieces slightly taller than the votive candle. Randomly hot glue the twigs around the candle about ½ to ¾ inch apart. Wrap raffia around the center and tie it in a bow. Glue dried flowers around the bow.

Terra Cotta Votive

Materials:

Sea sponge

Turquoise acrylic paint

1 4-inch clay flower pot

Raffia

Aquarium sand

Votive candle

Instructions: Dip the sponge into the paint. Lightly blot on paper, then on the pot. Do not cover the pot with paint; leave some of the natural color showing. Tie the raffia around the top into a bow. Fill with sand. Insert the votive candle in the sand.

Idea: Tie a piece of raffia around a 4-inch pillar candle. Tuck leaves and berries into the bow. This makes a quick and delightful gift.

SOUTHWESTERN PARTY FAVORS

In England, favors placed at each place setting are called "crackers," because they are cracked open revealing surprises inside. By filling his easy-to-make favors with Guatemalan

(Above) Give a Christmas gift that glows—Santa Fe candles. Photograph © by Joe Maggiore.

(Below) Bath Oils and Bath Salts. Photograph © by Joe Maggiore.

(Left) Southwestern Party Favors containing Guatemalan worry dolls, party hats, and special treats add fun to holiday tables. Photograph © by Joe Maggiore.

worry dolls, party hats, and assorted treats, Richard adapts this old European custom to Santa Fe celebrations.

According to legend, Guatemalan children tell one worry to each doll and put them under their pillow at night. In the morning, the dolls have taken their worries away.

Materials:

Crepe paper, in 2 colors

Cardboard toilet paper tubes

Party favors

Tacky craft glue (available at craft stores)

Raffia

Assorted small southwestern decorations

Tissue paper for paper hat and confetti

Instructions: Cut the crepe paper into 1 7 x 7-inch sheet and 1 7 x 9-inch sheet for each favor. Cut scallops on opposite ends of the crepe paper (pattern, page 128). Fill the tubes with favors. Wrap longer piece of crepe paper around the tube and glue the overlapping ends together. Repeat with small piece of paper. Tie raffia at the ends. Glue on decorations. Cut 2 pieces of tissue for paper hat (pattern, page 128) and glue ends together.

SANTA FE CHILE WRAP

Materials:

2 potatoes

Red acrylic paint

Small sponge

Mailing wrap paper, plain brown

Green acrylic paint

Instructions: Make a potato stamp by cutting ⅓ off the potato and (on the flat side) tracing the outline of a chile (see pattern, page 128). Cut away with a small paring knife to a thickness of ¼ inch. Repeat the process to make the stamp for the stem. Pour red acrylic paint into a small dish. Dab the sponge into the paint and dab the chile stamp. Test the stamp on blank paper before using. When using, gently rock the stamp to make sure the impression is clear. Repeat with the stem stamp, using green acrylic paint.

GIFT ON A GIFT

Materials:

Poster board

Assorted dried material

Mosses

Instructions: Cut a small circle about 3 to 4 inches in diameter out of poster board. Cluster assorted dried material in and around the focal point (Richard uses a *kachina* doll). Use dried material and mosses to fill in. Create a miniature scene to be removed from the gift package and used as a gift by itself. Now you have a gift on a gift.

(Below) Give your gifts a Santa Fe touch with handmade Christmas wrappings. Photograph © by Joe Maggiore.

(Pages 120–121) Full moon over the Inn at Loretto. Photograph © by Eduardo Fuss.

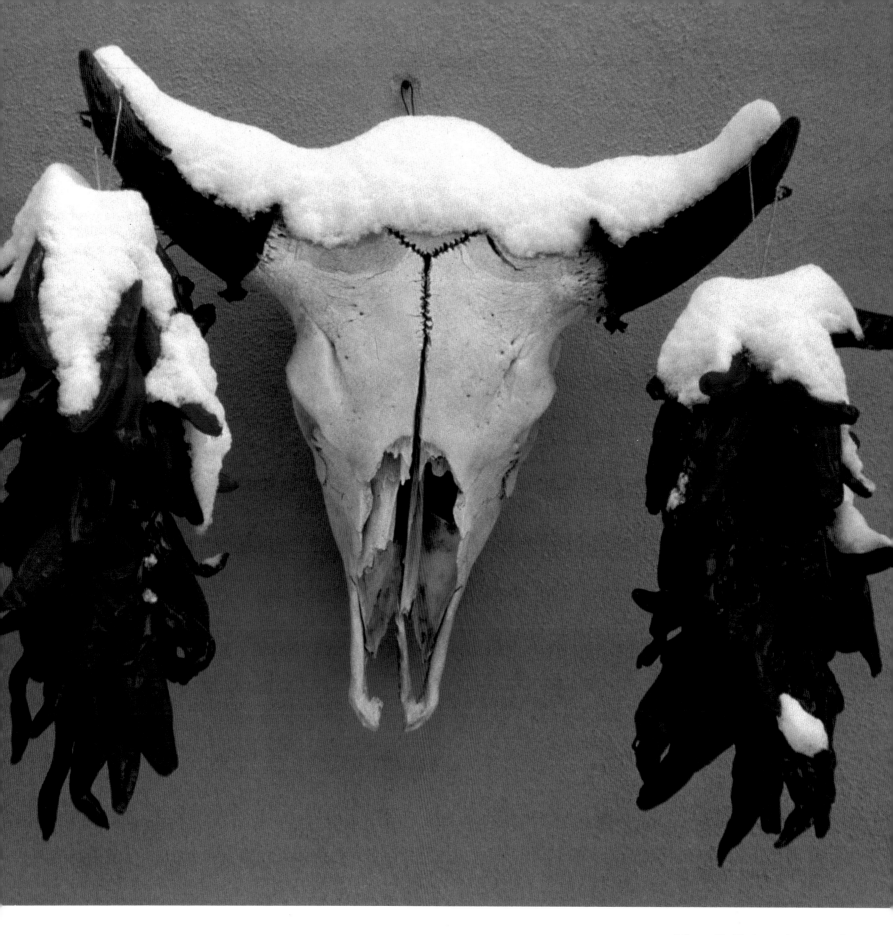

A Santa Fe Christmas image—red chile ristras hanging from a buffalo skull on an adobe wall. Photograph © by Scott Christopher.

Christmas Events

Santa Fe Concerts

Music has always played an important role in the celebration of Christmas. In Santa Fe the holiday season offers a wide variety of musical events ranging from traditional Christmas carols and folk music to the classics. Programs and times vary from year to year, so check with the following organizations for programs and schedules:

Santa Fe Symphony (505-983-3530)
Chamber Music Festival (505-983-2075)
Santa Fe Concert Association (505-984-8759)
Santa Fe Pro Musica (505-988-4640)
Santa Fe Desert Chorale (505-988-2282)
Sangre de Cristo Chorale (505-662-9717)

Santa Fe Area Celebrations

CHRISTMAS OPEN HOUSE IN MADRID

This picturesque turn-of-the-century mining town, located eighteen miles south of Santa Fe, has evolved from a ghost town into an arts and crafts community that goes all out with holiday decorations. The annual Christmas Open House with live music and refreshments in many galleries and shops is usually held early in December.

CHRISTMAS AT THE PALACE OF THE GOVERNORS

Live music, Santa Claus, storytelling, *bizcochitos*, and hot cider. Free. Donations of nonperishable food are welcome at the door (505-827-6474).

PLAZA PERFORMANCE OF LAS POSADAS

The Spanish-language reenactment of Mary and Joseph's search for shelter in Bethlehem before the birth of the Christ Child. It begins on the plaza and ends in the Palace of the Governors courtyard. Free: (505-827-6474).

LOS PASTORES

An ancient folk play in which the angels appear to the shepherds, usually performed before Christmas at the Museum of International Folk Art (505-827-6350).

CHRISTMAS EVE FAROLITO WALK DOWN CANYON ROAD

A Santa Fe tradition and experience that should not be missed. Thousands of *farolitos* line the street and decorate the art galleries, shops, and homes in this historic neighborhood. Locals and visitors alike gather around blazing *luminarias* to warm themselves and sing Christmas carols.

Check with the Santa Fe Chamber of Commerce for other holiday performances and events (505-988-3279).

Traditional Pueblo Winter Dances

The following is a list of pueblos near Santa Fe that traditionally perform public dances during the Christmas season. Because the specific dances vary from year to year and are often not set until just before the holidays, it is always best to call the pueblos for information.

Acoma: Located about fifty-six miles west of Albuquerque off I-40. Phone: 505-252-1139.

Isleta: Located thirteen miles south of Albuquerque off I-25. Phone: 505-869-3111.

Jemez: Located in the Jemez Mountains northwest of Bernalillo. Take N.M. 44 to San Ysidro and exit onto N.M. 4. Phone: 505-834-7359.

Laguna: Located forty-five miles west of Albuquerque off I-40. Phone: 505-552-6654 or 505-243-7616.

Nambe: Located eighteen miles north of Santa Fe. Turn off U.S. 84-285 at Pojoaque onto N.M. 503. Phone: 505-455-2036.

Picuris: Located sixty-five miles north of Santa Fe. Take the Dixon turnoff from N.M. 68 onto County Road 75. Phone: 505-587-2519.

Sandia: Located just north of Albuquerque on N.M. 313. Phone: 505-867-3317.

San Ildefonso: Located twenty-six miles north of Santa Fe, off N.M. 502, which leads to Los Alamos. Phone: 505-455-3549.

San Juan: Located four miles north of Española, off N.M. 68. Phone: 505-852-4400.

Santa Ana: Located northwest of Bernalillo on N.M. 44. Phone: 505-867-3301.

Santa Clara: Located three miles south of Española, off N.M. 30. Phone: 505-753-7326.

Santo Domingo: Located thirty miles south of Santa Fe, off I-25. Phone: 505-465-2214.

Taos: Located next to the city of Taos, sixty miles north of Santa Fe. Phone: 505-758-9593.

Tesuque: Located ten miles north of Santa Fe, off U.S. 84-285. Phone: 505-983-2667.

Zia: Located north of Bernalillo, off N.M. 44. Phone: 505-867-3304.

San Ildefonso dancer. Photograph © by David Salk.

Ski Santa Fe!

Christmas in Santa Fe also means first-rate skiing at the nearby Santa Fe Ski Area. Located just 16 miles northeast of Santa Fe in the Sangre de Cristo range of the Rocky Mountains, the ski area boasts varied terrain, short lift lines, a certified ski school, seven lifts, and some of the finest powder skiing in the United States.

Recently named one of the country's top 50 ski resorts in the category of upcoming areas, the Santa Fe Ski Area contains 550 acres, and averages a snow depth of 225 inches during the winter months. The area also boasts a 10,350 foot base with a vertical rise of another 1,650 feet—the view from the summit encompasses over 8,000 square miles.

The Santa Fe Ski Area features a special area for children, called Adventure Land. Designed to be explored on skis, Adventure Land features an obstacle course, a teepee, Rio Grande Roller Bumps, Pecos Gulch, and Billy the Kid's Cave.

Beginners ride their own chairlift and more advanced skiers take their pick of runs from wide-and-gentle to challenging moguls and glade skiing.

In addition to downhill skiing, the Sangre de Cristo Mountains offer a variety of cross country ski routes, tubing runs, and plenty of opportunities for snowshoeing. Phone 505-982-4429 for additional information.

Skiers flock to Santa Fe during the holidays to ski the flanks of the 12,000-foot-high Sangre de Cristo Mountains. With almost 600 acres inside its permit area, an average yearly snowfall of 225 inches, and 38 named trails, the Santa Fe Ski Area offers excellent slopes for beginner, intermediate, and advanced skiers. Cross-country skiers also have no difficulty finding the destination of their dreams in the Santa Fe area. Photograph © by Don Strehl.

Glossary

Adobo. *Carne adovada*; pork cooked in red chile sauce.

Atole. Cornmeal mush, served with honey.

Bizcochitos. Anise-flavored Christmas cookies.

Bulto. Statue of a saint, carved representation of a saint, often brightly painted and dressed in clothing.

Buñuelos. Chewy, deep-fried bread.

Chicos. Preserved corn, or hominy.

Chorizo. Spicy pork sausage.

Cocas. Little Spanish pizzas.

Empanaditas or Empanadas. Fried pastries filled with ground meat, piñon nuts, and spices.

Farolitos. Lanterns made of candles set in sand in paper bags. Traditionally used in Santa Fe at Christmas to decorate rooftops and pathways.

Feliz Navidad. Merry Christmas.

Horno. A beehive-shaped outdoor oven used by the Pueblo Indians and Spanish colonists.

Kachina dolls or figures. Carved, painted, and decorated figures representing Spirit Beings to the Pueblo Indians.

La Misa del Gallo. The Mass of the Rooster, or Midnight Mass.

La Noche Buena. Christmas Eve.

Las Posadas. A Spanish folk drama reenacting Mary and Joseph's search for shelter in Bethlehem.

Los Matachines. An exotic masked dance of Moorish-Spanish origin with roots in the history of the Spanish Conquest of Mexico. Performed on Christmas Day at Indian pueblos and Spanish villages in northern New Mexico.

Los Pastores. An ancient Christmas play in which angels appear to the shepherds.

Luminarias. Bonfires to light the way for Mary and Joseph on Christmas Eve.

Nacimientos. Manger scenes made of wood, straw, or pottery.

Pastelitos. Small pies made with dried fruit.

Piñata. A hollow papier mâché vessel made in various shapes and filled with candy and favors. The breaking of a *piñata* is traditionally a highlight of children's parties in Santa Fe.

Posole. Traditional Christmas stew made of pork and preserved corn, or hominy.

Reredos. Carved altarpiece.

Retablo. Religious image painted on wood.

Ristra. A string of chiles tied together and hung up to dry.

Santero. Maker of carved or painted representations of saints.

Santo. Saint; painted or carved representation of a saint.

Sopaipillas. Deep-fried puff pastries, served with butter and honey.

Tapas. Spanish for "little foods"; hors d'oeuvres.

Tomatillo. Small round green edible fruit of a Mexican ground cherry.

Skiers from all over the world come to the Santa Fe Ski Area, especially at Christmas time. Photograph © by Don Strel.

Resources & Bibliography

Resources

Adobo Catering, Santa Fe, New Mexico (505-989-7674).

Bandelier Environmental Papers (corrugated paper), Santa Fe, New Mexico (505-474-0900).

Boucher/Santa Fe Depot (handmade leather and tapastry clothing), Santa Fe, New Mexico (505-989-1131).

Caswell Massy (essential oils), San Francisco, California (415-681-1606).

The Chile Shop (southwestern kitchen and paper goods), Santa Fe, New Mexico (505-983-6080).

Cost Plus World Market (kitchen and paper goods, gourmet foods), Oakland, California (510-893-7300).

"The *Great Southwest* Chile Catalog" (chile specialties), Santa Fe, New Mexico (Mail Order: 1-800-GREAT-SW)

House of Hatten (Christmas decorations), Dallas, Texas (214-742-5568).

Jackalope (pottery, folk art), Santa Fe, New Mexico (505-471-8539).

Midwest Importors of Cannon Falls (Christmas decorations), Dallas, Texas (214-741-1401).

Nedra Matteucci's Fenn Galleries, Santa Fe, New Mexico (505-982-4631).

Pecos Valley Spice Co., Albuquerque, New Mexico (505-243-8297).

Pier I Imports (bath salts, kitchen and paper goods), Fort Worth, Texas (1-800-447-4371).

Polanco: A Gallery of Mexican Arts and Crafts, San Francisco, California (415-252-5753).

Pottery Barn (pottery accessories, decorations, candles), San Francisco, California (415-788-6810).

Sample House (gift wrap), Dallas, Texas (214-688-0751).

Santa Fe Vineyards Winery, Santa Fe, New Mexico (505-982-3474).

The Shop (Christmas ornaments and decorations), Santa Fe, New Mexico (505-983-4823).

Susan's Christmas Shop (Christmas ornaments and decorations), Santa Fe, New Mexico (505-983-2127).

Bibliography

Baca, Elmo. *Santa Fe Fantasy: Quest for the Golden City.* Santa Fe, N.M.: Clear Light Publishers, 1994.

Collier, John. *The Rites and Ceremonies of the Indians of the Southwest.* N.Y.: Barnes and Noble Books, 1993.

Ellis, Richard N. *New Mexico: Past and Present.* Albuquerque: University of New Mexico Press, 1971.

Fergusson, Erna. *Dancing Gods: Indian Ceremonials of New Mexico and Arizona.* Albuquerque: University of New Mexico Press, 1931.

——. *New Mexico: A Pageant of Three Peoples.* Albuquerque: University of New Mexico Press, 1951.

Foley, Daniel J. *Christmas the World Over.* Randor, Pa.: Chilton Book Company, 1963.

Hazen-Hammond, Susan. *A Short History of Santa Fe.* San Francisco: Lexikos, 1988.

Ortega, Pedro Ribera. *Christmas in Old Santa Fe.* Santa Fe, N.M.: Sunstone Press, 1973.

Sando, Joe S. *Pueblo Nations: Eight Centuries of Pueblo Indian History.* Santa Fe, N.M.: Clear Light Publishers, 1992.

Craft & Gift Food Patterns

Shown 50% of actual size

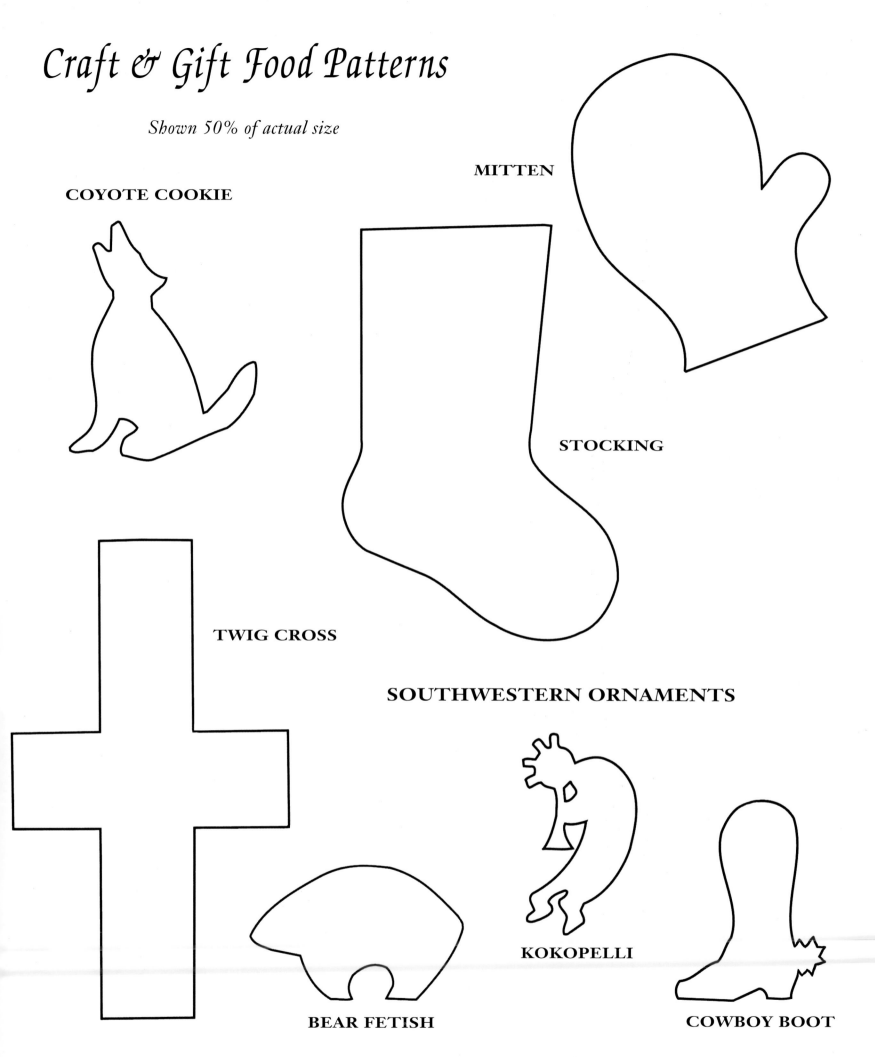

COYOTE COOKIE

MITTEN

STOCKING

TWIG CROSS

SOUTHWESTERN ORNAMENTS

KOKOPELLI

BEAR FETISH

COWBOY BOOT

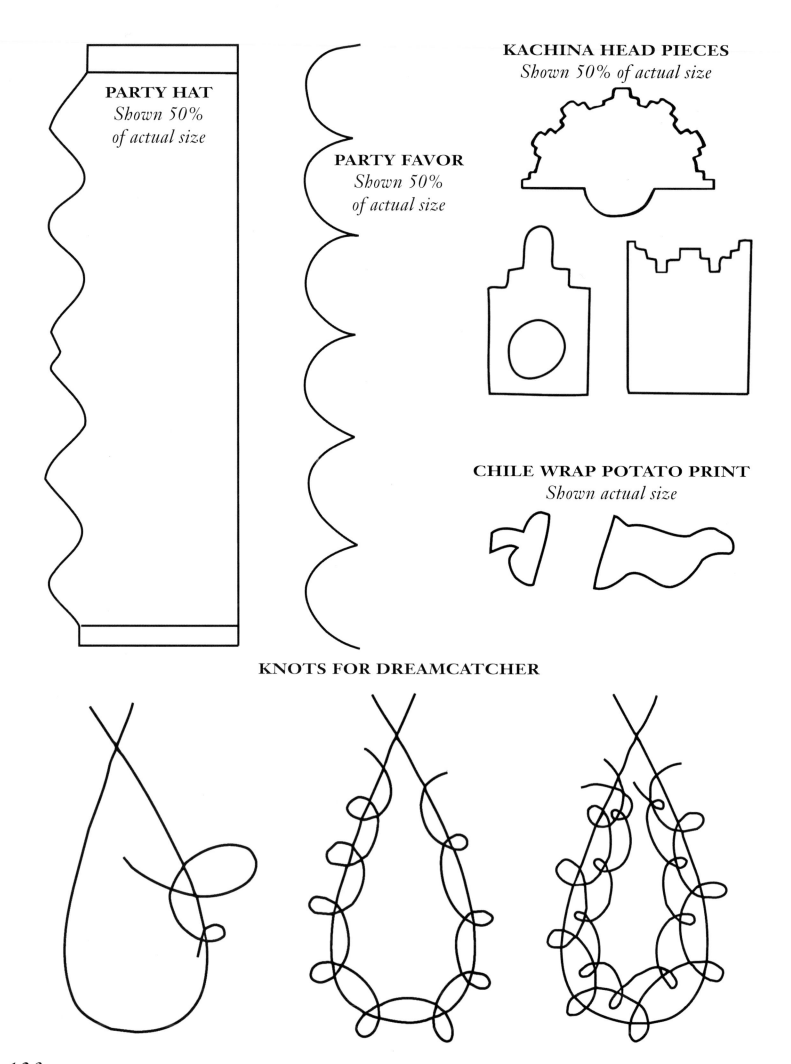

PARTY HAT
Shown 50% of actual size

PARTY FAVOR
Shown 50% of actual size

KACHINA HEAD PIECES
Shown 50% of actual size

CHILE WRAP POTATO PRINT
Shown actual size

KNOTS FOR DREAMCATCHER